THE HERAL
DIARY

THE HERALD DIARY

Fur Goodness' Sake!

Ken Smith

BLACK & WHITE PUBLISHING

First published 2013
by Black & White Publishing Ltd
29 Ocean Drive, Edinburgh EH6 6JL

1 3 5 7 9 10 8 6 4 2   13 14 15 16

ISBN: 978 1 84502 705 6

A CIP catalogue record for this book is available from the British Library.

Typeset by Iolaire Typesetting, Newtonmore
Printed and bound by Grafica Veneta S. p. A. Italy

Contents

Introduction

What a year it has been. Horsemeat in burgers, the Royal Family never out of the news, Rangers still in the mire, oh and Scots thinking about running their own country. What's not to laugh about?

Fortunately when Scots do laugh at themselves they send their stories to *The Herald* newspaper's Diary column rather than keep it to themselves.

These are our favourites which we hope will bring a smile to your lips.

1
Glasgow

Some of our best stories come, of course, from Glasgow.

NEWS that people are spending less money on home improvements reminds us of the Glasgow council official visiting a house in Blackhill, where he noted that the tenant had knocked through archways in all the rooms so that you could travel from the living room to the kitchen to the bedroom and back round to the living room.

When asked why he had done so, he replied: "To train my greyhound."

PEOPLE take up hobbies for a variety of reasons. Gerry McCulloch was in a camera shop in Glasgow's Merchant City discussing the merits of a telescopic lens with the assistant when the door burst open. "Haw Jimmy!" announced the new arrival. "Ah've just gied up the drink an' ah'm lookin' fir another hobby. Oany cheap camras?"

GLASGOW – not a place for exuberance.

Riverside, the new transport museum, has just been named European Museum of the Year. The staff immediately put this news on its Facebook page expecting, no doubt, many messages of congratulations. But amongst the first to comment was a visitor who merely wrote: "Kelvin Hall was better."

BUS company First Glasgow has changed the numbering of some services to tidy things up a bit, so that the 44 is now the 4. Andy Cumming was on the now 4 into the city centre when a passenger got on and told the driver: "What number is this bus? Wan of yer fours is missing."

When the driver tried to explain, the passenger asked: "Still go the same route as a 44?" When the driver answered in the affirmative, the passenger told him: "Aye well, it's a 44 then," and triumphantly made his way on board.

KATE WOODS in Colorado tells us she was having tea with her cousin some years ago in a posh Glasgow tearoom and they were looking at the items in an auction catalogue.

Says Kate: "We were sharing the table with an elegant elderly lady who looked at the catalogue and told us, 'Antiques, my dear? Why, we threw better things out of the maid's room years ago.'"

WE were drawn to a bulletin board which asked folk what was the weirdest thing they had seen in Glasgow. We liked the tale of the chap driving along Alexandra Parade who saw a tramp sitting at a bus stop eating chips. When a jogger ran past, the tramp chased after her shouting: "Have one! You know you want to!" Added the driver: "The best of it was that she had her headphones on. She must have been the only one who was completely oblivious to the guy."

STREET mendicants in Glasgow are usually a pitiful sight, sitting on a piece of cardboard, asking for change from passers-by.

However a Glasgow reader tells us he was walking past one such beggar when the person in front of him told the chap: "Sorry," and kept on walking.

The chap sitting on the pavement shouted after him: "Aye, I'll be sorry too when I've got money."

GLASGOW has apparently been named the UK's most violent city. We don't know if there is any connection but the Glasgow firm of defence lawyers Livingstone Brown posted on its Twitter account yesterday, one imagines with a sorrowful shake of the head: "Defence witness comes in to court to give evidence today with the slogan Weekend Offender on his jumper."

DIFFICULT questions children ask: a reader was in Glasgow's Sauchiehall Street when a father was passing a takeaway shop specialising in chicken dishes with his young son who asked: "Why do they have to kill chickens?" Perhaps his dad was fed up answering too many questions as he merely replied: "Because chickens are man's natural enemy," and kept on walking.

A DELIVERY man swears to us he knocked on a door in Glasgow's South Side and told the chap who answered: "I've got a parcel for your next-door neighbour." The puzzled chap replied: "You've come to the wrong house then."

THE SUBWAY in Glasgow is called either the subway or the underground – but never the tube. As comedy actor Sanjeev Kohli told some southerners: "In Glasgow 'travelling by tube' means getting a piggy back off an imbecile."

NOT EVERYONE in Glasgow believes it is the most attractive of cities. As Ronnie Scott argues: "They are building a sheltered housing complex for ex-servicemen in Cranhill near my home. I'm concerned about the location as it's bound to bring back memories of downtown Basra."

WE MENTIONED the sculpture exhibition at Glasgow's Gallery of Modern Art which is a tad avant-garde. Referring to one exhibit that features ceramic orange peel scattered across the floor, someone wrote in the gallery's comments book: "I felt my OCD kicking off, and I had to leave before I started tidying up."

OUR NOSTALGIC mention of Milanda bread reminds Jim Scott of being on a bus in Duke Street near the former Milanda Bakery when a youth got on wearing overalls with the slogan: "Mother's Pride" stitched on it. The driver nodded at the badge and asked the chap: "Are you?"

JOURNALIST Nuala Naughton is compiling stories about Glasgow's famous Barrowland Ballroom, which became one of the city's best live music venues. A chap was showing Nuala his collection of ticket stubs, and she remarked that she never knew the Birmingham group UB40 had been a support act so often.

"No," the chap explained, "they stamped 'with UB40' on the tickets when you got a discount for being unemployed."

WE MENTIONED Glasgow being named a top tourist destination in Britain. Deedee Cuddihy was walking down Sauchiehall Street when she spotted some tourists taking a picture of something on the pavement outside a fast food shop. Curious as to what had attracted their attention, Deedee went over – and saw it was a set of false teeth that had somehow ended up outside the shop.

MEANWHILE in Glasgow, the smell of barbecues was everywhere. It reminds us of when Tim Vine won a comedy award at the Edinburgh Fringe. On receiving his prize, Tim declared: "I'm going to celebrate by going to Sooty's barbecue and having a sweepsteak."

WE HEAR of a classic Glasgow moment outside the City Chambers when about 30 pensioners clambered on to a coach that they thought would take them to Largs to catch the *Waverley*. For various reasons they failed to notice that a) the coach was left-hand-drive b) the wording on its flank was in German and c) the bus company's address was in Austria.

Strenuous efforts are made to claim certain seats, but firm resistance is encountered. Voices are raised. Elbows are used. An eyewitness translates, for the benefit of the newcomers, something said by a passenger – "We're going to Vienna!" Pause. One loud newcomer digests this and says: "So this bus isnae gaun tae Largs, then?"

A CHAP about to take a drink in a Glasgow pub was interrupted by the toper next to him who said: "I wouldn't touch that Tennent's Lager if I were you – it'll make your teeth fall out."

"Why would that happen?" asked the puzzled chap. "Because it's mine," the toper replied.

A MEMBER of staff at a major power company tells us colleagues from Newcastle attended a training day in Glasgow, wearing their company's bright yellow high-viz jackets on which was printed "Challenge me," reflecting the company's culture of challenging unsafe behaviour.

One of the chaps returned from a stroll around the city centre and asked what the "square go" was that a local youth had shouted at him.

IT IS CHINESE New Year, which reminds us of the Chinese gentlemen many years ago trying to hail a taxi on Woodlands Road, at Chinese New Year, encumbered with a carry-out and two crates of oranges. A passer-by showed impressive knowledge of chronology for a February night by telling them: "Aye it's murder trying to get a taxi in Glasgow at New Year."

THE DAFT news story about the supposed lion spotted in Essex brings forth from reader Gerry MacKenzie the hoary old gag: "It reminded me of the two lions strolling down Sauchiehall Street. One remarked to the other, 'Jings, it's quiet for a Saturday afternoon!'"

EXPAT Jim Farrell, now living in Ontario, Canada, returned to Scotland for a visit, and due to the good weather was strolling around Glasgow in shorts and sandals. As he had been spending quite a time golfing in the sunshine in Canada, his legs were tanned but his ankles white from where he had been wearing his golf shoes.

Says Jim: "Exiting Queen Street Station, I was spotted by one young girl who said to her pal: 'Look at that silly old man – he painted his tan on, and forgot to do his ankles.'

"Glasgow at its finest."

THE WEBSITE Google maps allows you to leave reviews of businesses that appear on its maps, so some inventive chaps have left reviews on the Glasgow map of the city's Barlinnie Jail.

Writes one allegedly former incumbent, in the style of a holiday review: "10/10. Best vacation I've ever had! This place is so exclusive that you need to get a judge to recommend you! The employees there don't seem to want you to leave.

"They show you to your room as soon as you arrive and make sure you get the finest shower when you get there."

Still wouldn't want to stay there though.

INEVITABLY our search for nicknames has wandered into the bizarre. Steve Brennan in Lanarkshire's Glenmavis tells us: "There was a wee Glaswegian nicknamed Jimmy The Coupon. He went out every Saturday and somebody filled him in."

WE ARE still trying to track down which comic was describing an appearance in Glasgow and recounted: "The act on stage before me was so bad that the crowd was still booing him halfway through my act."

SCRAMBLES. A reader tells us of a chap in Rothesay, the owner of a local shop some years ago, who was getting married for the fourth time. As the wedding car left the church, he wound down the window and threw out a bundle of one-pound notes. Recalls our reader: "As the car sped away, so did the pound notes, which the crowd were frantically trying to grab.

"It turned out that our groom had tied them with threads and had not let go."

SCRAMBLE stories continue with Alan Duncan going even further back in time to back-court singers in Govan who serenaded windows in the hope of a few pennies being thrown out to them.

Alan says there was the occasional tenant who, if they didn't like the quality of the singing, would heat up a couple of pennies first before throwing them out, in the hope of watching poor performers reacting badly to their fingers being scorched.

CORA SNYDER tells us: "Another cruel trick I remember we used to pull on back-court singers – wrap an old penny in the silver paper off your bar of chocolate before you lob it out the window, and watch them scramble hastily after it, thinking it's half-a-crown."

A LATE-NIGHT reveller in Glasgow couldn't fault the logic of the young girl serving in the chip shop last weekend when he asked for a bag of chips and she inquired if he wanted regular or large. Not sure of the quantities involved, he asked what the difference was. "You get mair chips," she replied.

2
Relationships

Internet dating has brought a modern slant to relationships, but the same old pitfalls remain.

A POLLOKSHIELDS reader tells us she was asking a girlfriend how her meeting with a chap from an internet dating site had gone. Her pal replied: "It was quite clear that the long romantic walks he talked about on his profile were mainly to the fridge."

JOHN PARK hears a bemused chap in the pub look at his mobile phone and announce: "I've just received a blank text from my wife."
   "Is she still not talking to you?" asked his mate.

NOSTALGIA alert! Our mention of the sex and bondage novel *Fifty Shades of Grey* reminds Jim Hair of the gag by the great variety hall comedian Lex McLean who told his Glasgow Pavilion audience: "Told the wife that black underwear turned me on.
   "So she didn't wash my vest for a month."

FATHER'S DAY, and as comedian Gary Delaney, who is appearing at the Edinburgh Fringe, commented: "Wondering who gave you a card on Valentine's Day? Good. Wondering who gave you a card on Father's Day? Bad."

A GLASGOW reader tells us she held her breath when her young daughter peered keenly into the face of her unmarried aunt and asked: "Why have you so many laughter lines?" Auntie, though, merely replied: "It must be all the clowns I've dated."

THE DIFFICULTIES of legislating for same-sex marriages was being discussed at an Ayrshire golf club where one of the stalwarts sadly opined: "I'm more in favour of some sex marriages."

A READER out with colleagues at the office party heard the office maintenance man announce: "I've been banned from all major football grounds in Scotland for a year." As staff tried to digest this nugget he then added: "That'll teach me to forget our wedding anniversary."

OFFICE PARTIES continued. A west-end reader heard two young chaps holding a post-mortem on their office do, at which partners were also invited. "I wasn't that drunk," one of them insisted. But his pal reminded him: "So how come you ended up asking your girlfriend if she was single."

AN EDINBURGH reader phones about the news that Edinburgh Zoo pandas Tian Tian and Yang Guang have failed to mate, and tells us: "It's Edinburgh.

"Someone needed to explain to him that he should have bragged about his property portfolio and bought her buckets of champagne first. Then it wouldn't have been a problem."

A WORKER at an insurance call-centre in Lanarkshire tells us he was dealing with a customer who was wanting car insurance for himself and his girlfriend but was surprised by how high the quote was. Trying to lighten the moment, the call-centre worker told him it would be cheaper if they were married.

After a pause, the caller replied: "Maybe so. But you don't buy an airline just to get a free packet of peanuts." Which we think means he's not planning to get married any day soon.

A READER swears to us he was in a boisterous city-centre bar where he heard a woman tell her pals: "I just wish more of my handcuff stories involved boyfriends and no' the polis."

A MILNGAVIE reader tells us he was out for a walk at the start of the West Highland Way when he came across a tree which had two sets of initials carved inside a crude heart shape, and he realised he hadn't seen such an old-fashioned way of professing your love for someone in years.

As he tells us: "I wish I could remember the comedian who told his audience, 'When I see lovers' names carved into a tree, I don't think it's cute – I just think it's strange how many people take knives on a date.'"

CHAP in the pub told his pals: "I asked my wife what women really want, and she said it was 'attentive lovers.'

"Or maybe it was a tent of lovers. I wasn't really listening."

THE CHAP in a Glasgow pub at the weekend declared to his pals: "I overheard the girlfriend on the phone to her pal saying she wants to get engaged on her birthday. I hope she finds someone nice."

SOME RELATIONSHIPS sound as if they might not last. A reader in a Lanarkshire pub heard the chap further up the bar impatiently answer his mobile phone with: "I told you I'd be there in five minutes. Stop calling me every ten minutes to check."

THE THINGS taxi drivers hear. Former part-time Glasgow cabbie Jimmy Higgins recalls taking a group of six women, aged between 20 and 50, to a city centre restaurant.

They began discussing plans for the rest of the night and agreed to go on to a club. Several potential clubs were discarded before the oldest woman mentioned Madness, in Bothwell Street.

The suggestion was howled down by her younger friends. One said: "Madness, it's full of seedy auld men."

To which the older woman responded: "They might be seedy auld men tae you, but they're prospects tae me."

"THE WIFE accused me of ruining her birthday yesterday," said the chap in the pub. "I told her that couldn't be right as I hadn't even remembered it was her birthday."

SOME Glasgow ladies were discussing their husbands this week when one opined: "My husband always tells me he could have had any woman he pleased – he just couldn't please any."

TAKING a brave pill is reader Martin Morrison who swears to us: "A parcel arrived containing shoes for our three-year-old daughter. They were a bit big, but her mum told her, 'Don't worry. You'll grow into them.'

"The next day a pair of trousers arrived for my wife. To my wife's annoyance, these were also a size too large. So I offered my wife the same reassurance she'd given our wee girl. Well, blow me. Talk about inconsistent."

A READER out socialisng in Glasgow's city centre at the weekend was impressed by the insouciance of the chap in the bar who was asked by the young woman he was talking to: "What would you do if you had a million pounds in the bank?" The chap merely replied: "Wonder where the rest of it had got to."

IT WAS St Valentine's Day, but not every Glaswegian is a smooth romantic. A Glasgow woman in her 40s tells us she was in a west-end bar at the weekend when a chap came up and thought she would be impressed with his opening line: "Well, here I am. What were your other two wishes?"

WE URGED you on St Valentine's Day not to make the mistake of the hubby last year who announced: "The wife says she doesn't want much for Valentine's Day – just some chocolates and a few little surprises."

He then added: "So Kinder Eggs it is, then."

KATE WOODS overhears a group of women of a certain age discussing a widowed friend who had met a "new man".

One of them disclosed that she had been bold enough to ask the widow how intimate the relationship had become.

The lady had given the memorable reply: "Well let me put it this way – it's the middle of winter but my legs are shaved."

A READER swears to us that a young woman on his bus into Glasgow told a pal: "Tricky business, dating. It's hard to tell how old anyone is these days. I've made some schoolboy errors."

FOOTBALL impressionist Paul Reid loves Dundee, where he works. He told a fundraising dinner that Las Vegas should be twinned with Dundee, "as they're the only two cities where girls date you for chips."

He might not have used the word date.

MORE INTERNET dating stories: we hear from one chap who met a woman in a Glasgow bar after chatting online, and after some desultory conversation she announced she had to go to the loo. Nothing strange about that, he thought, until she added that she hated using public toilets, so she would have to go home.

She left him there, and never contacted him again, before it eventually dawned on him that she really did not like his company.

A READER heard a woman out with her pals in Glasgow's west end being asked by them how she was coping with her husband being down in London on business for a week. "I'm in a deep depression," she explained. "Why's that?" asked a worried pal.

"I'm sleeping on his side of the bed."

A BIT parky as Jimmy Manson in Ayr tells us: "The other morning my wife said, 'I'm going out to scrape the car.'

"'Against what?' I replied."

THE PUB is of course one of the most popular spots for meeting the opposite sex. Jamie McGarry in Rhu watched a couple of chaps at the pub he was in approach two ladies, with one of the lads introducing his pal as "Mr Duvet". Says Jamie: "'That's an odd name', was the reply from one of the ladies. 'Why do you call him that?' The instant response was: 'He's been turned down more times than a hotel bed.'"

INTERNET dating sites are all the rage just now. A Glasgow woman relays to us that she felt compelled to say to the chap she met online when they finally met in person for a meal: "You don't get out much do you?" The reason for her question was when she ordered scallops, and they arrived in a scallop shell, her date remarked: "That's disgusting. They've served it in an ashtray."

WE LIKED the line from divorced stand-up Maxine Jones, who appeared at the Glasgow Comedy Festival, about bringing up her sons after separating from her husband. Said Maxine: "Quite hard bringing up three boys. Basically, you're rearing three replicas of someone you don't like very much."

OFFICE PARTY season, and a Glasgow reader tells us about a young woman in his office, perhaps having imbibed too much, who was discussing her ex-boyfriend with other women from the office.

She told them: "He texted 'Stop calling me.' I just wonder what he really means by that.

"Do you think I should phone and ask him?"

DATING, and the chap who was nicknamed Mr Duvet as women turned him down so often, reminds Douglas McLeod of the chap called The Sledge by his pals as on nights out he was always getting pulled by dogs.

THEATRE company By The Slice, which put on the play *Call Me!* at the Edinburgh Fringe about dating disasters, is collecting stories to freshen up the play.

One chap in Edinburgh told them a first date didn't go well when the conversation dried up.

The dullest point, he told them, was "when I ended up asking her whether she made sandwiches for work in the morning or the night before."

TIS THE SEASON of endless shopping, and Peter Drummond receives an email from the British Red Cross which states: "Give a gift of first aid training courses this Christmas." Says Peter: "If I were to give someone that as a present, then I suspect I would shortly thereafter be in need of first aid myself."

WOMEN, it has to be admitted, can be a bit sharp-tounged about their contemporaries. A Hyndland reader says he heard two women discussing a mutual friend who had apparently dated quite a few chaps in recent years.

"I wouldn't say she takes a lot of men home," said one. "But her bedroom is listed on TripAdvisor."

YES, folk were having a great time at Glasgow pubs on Hogmanay. One chap in a west-end bar told a young woman he could tell her what day she was born if she gave him a passionate kiss. After being locked in an embrace, he came up for air and told her: "Yesterday."

WE MENTIONED saying the wrong thing at the wrong time. A Paisley reader said his wife was moaning about something trivial he had forgotten to do, when he told her: "You sound like my ex-wife." His shocked spouse told him he had never said he had been married before. "I haven't," he told her.

A CHAP in a Glasgow pub was being quizzed by his mates about his use of a popular online dating site. "I put down that I was looking for a woman who loves long walks on the beach," he told them. "It'll give her something to do while I watch the fitba."

MORE Glasgow pub chat. The other night a chap said he made the fatal mistake of suggesting to his wife that she had perhaps put on a pound or two over the festive season. He confessed that she quickly riposted: "That's rich coming from someone who needs sat-nav to do up his trouser belt."

A FEMALE reader phones to ask us: "Have you seen the astonishing pictures of Mars beamed back by Nasa's Curiosity rover? Not a pair of socks, empty beer cans or TV remotes in sight. So much for that book which claimed that men are from Mars."

A BEARSDEN reader points out the different thinking processes between men and women by telling us he got home from work and told his wife: "Alison in the office was showing pictures of her new baby on her phone."

When his wife asked: "What did she have?" he responded: "A Samsung Galaxy," before he realised what she meant.

THE MOSCOW State Circus visited Braehead. A reader swears to us that the woman next to him at the show was watching the acrobats on the trapeze when she said to her husband: "You'd never catch me doing that."

"I wouldn't even try," he replied.

THE DESULTORY conversation in a Glasgow bar at the weekend was enlivened by one chap declaring: "The wife had a funny dream last night. She dreamed she'd married a millionaire."

"You're lucky," said a customer further up the bar. "Mine dreams that in the daytime."

"MY HUSBAND had a near-death experience at the weekend," a woman was heard telling her pals in Glasgow's west end yesterday. "He tried to change the channel when *Strictly Come Dancing* was on."

3
Doon the Coast

Lots of Glasgow folk retire to Ayrshire, which is perhaps why we had so many stories from down the coast.

FINALLY everything's started to click," announced the old chap in the Ayrshire golf club. "My knees, my elbows, my neck."

WEEKEND sunshine brought out golfers for the first time in months. An Ayrshire club member says a retired chap joined his club and told the professional his handicap was a respectable six, and his main difficulty was getting out of bunkers.

The pro said he could teach him some useful ways of improving his bunker play but the chap added: "No, son. I mean climbing oot the bunker after I've taken my shot."

GORDON LAW was at the Irvine Meadow v Cumnock Junior Cup tie when he heard the Irvine Meadow manager shout to his own striker: "Stop fouling!" He was impressed by the sportsmanship until the chap next to him explained: "That's junior football talk meaning, 'Stop getting caught fouling by the ref.'"

A BIG crowd watched the time trials of the British Cycling National Road Championships in Stewarton, Ayrshire, and the announcer tried to get some rivalry going between those gathered at the top and bottom of the hill by seeing who could cheer the loudest.

Among the banter being shouted between the two crowds was the chap at the top of the hill who bawled: "While youse are aw doon there, ma brother is tanning yer hooses."

HAVE YOU ever done any after-dinner speaking?" a senior member of an Ayrshire golf club was asked last week. "Yes," he replied. "Occasionally I ask my wife if she'd like me to do the dishes."

SOME SENIOR golfers at an Ayrshire golf club were having a post-round drink when one asked: "Do you ever go into a room and forget why you went there?" A fellow member immediately replied: "That's why Davie lost his job as a firefighter."

JANETTE WHITE from Kilmarnock has been reminiscing with other folk from the town on Facebook about the good old days. She tells us: "Someone recalled when the Mormons went into a notorious part of Kilmarnock and offered to take a crowd of youngsters swimming. This being a rare treat, they jumped at the chance and were duly taken to Kilmarnock Baths.

"A few weeks later, they all received baptism certificates through the post."

WE MENTIONED inter-village insults in Ayrshire. Annabel Taylor tells us: "They say that in Drongan they stand the dead in the bus shelters to make the place look busy."

THE FORMER mining town of New Cumnock in Ayrshire was named Scotland's most dismal town. When it was runner-up in a similar competition a few years back someone suggested the community council put up a sign on the outskirts of the village saying: "Don't laugh yet . . . wait until you see Cumnock."

ARRAN having its power restored reminded Jim Arnold in Whiting Bay of his agitated father waiting up for Jim's brother who was late home from a dance many years ago. Says Jim: "There was a knock on the door from the local Hydro Board engineer who said: 'I've been called out to a power failure in Whiting Bay, but I cannot understand why your lights are on when everyone else's are not.'

"This was too much for dad who exploded, 'That's because everyone else is in their ruddy bed and we're still up waiting for a dancing teenager to come home!'"

OUR STORY about folk in New Cumnock criticising Cumnock is just one of many examples of intervillage rivalries in Ayrshire. Grant Young recalls a Burns supper speaker making the disparaging comment on Auchinleck: "Where even the horses are up on bricks."

AN apocryphal story from Ayrshire where we are told about a millionaire businessman who has a helicopter to speed him around his empire. Recently, having cut the grass on his estate with his ride-on mower, he thought he would blow the cut grass away by hovering over it.

His wife, hearing the noise of the helicopter opened the door to find out what was going on – and ended up head to foot covered in grass, and with a lawn where the carpet used to be.

THE CLOCKS went back. As one chap in an Ayrshire golf club announced: "My phone, television and laptop all put their clocks back an hour without me touching them. So now I'm not even as smart as the stuff I own."

"EVEN AFTER 20 years of marriage, my wife's still a real good looker," said a chap in another Ayrshire golf club. "No matter where I lose my keys, she can always find them."

A DISCUSSION on smoking was taking place at the golf club when one chap declared to a smoker: "So what is it now, eight quid a packet? At a packet a day that's nearly three grand a year. So over 20 years you could have bought an F-Type Jaguar."

"Do you smoke?" the smoker replied.

"No," said the chap.

"So where's your Jag?" asked the smoker.

4
Banning the Bond Villian

Celebrities still have a fascination for Scots – even if it's just to take the mickey out of them.

BIG cinema hit in Glasgow was the new Bond film *Skyfall*. The Spanish actor Javier Bardem, playing the Bond villain, has sparked the latest 007 gag. "I've thrown the new Bond villain out of my pub." "Javier Bardem?" "No, he can come back when he's sober."

GOOD to see that comedian Billy Connolly has not forgotten his Glasgow upbringing despite moving to America. His wife Pamela Stephenson, speaking in Australia, was telling her audience what Billy told her when she said she wanted to go on last year's *Strictly Come Dancing*.

In what must have been said by many Glasgow husbands over the years, Billy urged her not to go on because "you'll make an a*** of yourself'".

BBC Scotland soap *River City* is 10 years old, and has provided work for hundreds of actors over the years. It reminds us of the Scottish actor meeting a fellow thespian in a West End bar and asking him if he had done any theatrical work recently. "It's been four years since my last role," he replied. Sympathising, his mate told him: "Mine was nearly three years ago." He then added: "One of these days we've got to get out of this business."

WE mentioned the collection of writings by legendary *Herald* editor Arnold Kemp entitled *Confusion To Our Enemies*. A story Arnold always told against himself was when he was invited to a reception at Buckingham Palace, and was phoned beforehand to be told that Princess Margaret was frightfully keen to meet him.

As it took Arnold more than an hour to find her, he pushed rather impatiently past her acolytes and brusquely announced: "Your Royal Highness, I believe you wanted to speak to me."
After a lengthy frigid silence, she eventually told Arnold: "I say, would you mind fetching me an ashtray?"

OUR tales of legendary Scots journalist Arnold Kemp remind novelist Meg Henderson of when boisterous Scotland fans climbed onto the goalpost at Wembley after a rare victory and dug up parts of the pitch as souvenirs. Says Meg: "Arnold called the gentlemanly Hector Munro, Scottish MP and Tory sports spokesman for a comment.

"Hector was ecstatic, said, 'Good for them! Tell them to bring me back a lump!' A few minutes later Hector's wife called and said what Hector had meant to say was, 'This kind of thuggish behaviour disgraces Scotland and must be stopped.'

"Arnold, being a gentleman, published her version."

A HIGHLIGHT at Celtic Connections was veteran politician Tony Benn introducing the film about his career, Will and Testament. Tony tells of driving near Westminster many years ago when he had an urgent need to go to the loo. In desperation he lifted the bonnet of the car, and relieved himself over the engine, hoping he would be out of public sight.

However a passer-by stopped and told him: "I see your problem – your radiator's leaking."

OUR mention of Max Bygraves at the Glasgow Empire reminds a reader of Roy Castle recalling playing the Empire in the 1950s when he and Jimmy James were supporting Slim Whitman. Said Roy: "They started hissing all the way from the Royal Circle to the stalls. Then the slow clap began. We went through an 18-minute spot in four minutes without leaving a word out.

"We came off and Slim said: 'Hey, what's going on here?' Jimmy replied: 'You are.'"

THE story of the musical *Jesus Christ Superstar* in Glasgow provokes Robin Gilmour in Milngavie to claim that when the show was previously in the city it followed on at the theatre after Sydney Devine. The handyman putting up the sign left up "Sydney Devine" and put beside it "Superstar" then below it "Jesus Christ".

GLASGOW band Deacon Blue are back touring, 25 years after their first album. Ronnie Buchanan in Larkhall tells us his brother-in-law was in the gents during the break at their concert last week, when two well-dressed ladies appeared saying they weren't waiting in the lengthy queue at the ladies.

Says Ronnie: "A cubicle was duly made available and they both squeezed in. In the confused silence that followed a lone male voice shouted, 'Mind ladies when yer done, leave the seat up.'"

WELL done Celtic winning the league. Singer Rod Stewart tells in his autobiography of the madness of being a Celtic fan. He was in Vancouver and was heading to a bar at four in the morning to see a Celtic game due to the time difference. Wrote Rod: "The sun was just coming up, and I saw this bloke on his bicycle, with his cycle clips on, in his hooped Celtic shirt, pedalling determinedly through the empty streets, and I thought, 'You and me both, pal.'"

TEXAN country singer Kinky Friedman returns for a gig in Glasgow in April. Mike Ritchie, who heard the humorous Kinky at his last Glasgow concert, tells us Kinky told the audience of a Texas oil baron who was praying for divine intervention as the oil was drying up and his 10 Cadillacs were off the road. Praying beside him was a Mexican farm worker, desperate for money as his wife was pregnant and he had just lost his job. Annoyed at the interference, the Texan took $100 out his pocket, handed it to the Mexican, and told him not to bother God with all that rubbish.

GLASGOW'S Dean Park, who has played panto dames with great success for nearly 30 years, is one of the stars this year in The Wizard of Never Woz at Glasgow's Pavilion. His first dame appearance was in Inverness in the 1980s. He was sitting in his dressing room then, with full make-up, huge fake boobs and tights on when his parents came to see him. His father, of traditional West of Scotland stock, took in the scene and asked Dean: "Is this what it's come to, son?"

WE mentioned panto dame Dean Park appearing at the Glasgow Pavilion's The Wizard of Never Woz this year. We recall Dean in an earlier Pavilion Panto, Jack and the Beanstalk, when he was inside a fake cottage which was essentially a box on wheels. The brakes failed, and it started moving downstage towards the orchestra pit. The musicians hurriedly grabbed their instruments and fled, while stage hands frantically grabbed at the back of the box, stopping it tumbling into the pit with a perturbed Dean inside.

Afterwards legendary performer Jack Milroy told Dean in the bar: "You'll need to keep that bit in the show, son. It was brilliant."

BRITISH heavyweight Audley Harrison suffered an embarrassing defeat when he was knocked out after just 70 seconds in his latest fight. Naturally there are a few jokes circulating about poor Audley but as a reader warns us: "I don't think you should tell any Audley Harrison jokes – I'm pretty sure even a punchline would actually knock Audley out these days."

FORMER Rangers star Willie Henderson told Epilepsy Scotland's charity dinner in Glasgow that when Billy McNeill was Celtic manager he told feisty midfielder Peter Grant before a crucial Old Firm game to go out and kick lumps out of opponent Graeme Souness.

Billy then added to a crestfallen Peter: "Don't worry about being sent off. They'll miss him more than we'll miss you."

A fellow speaker at the dinner, snooker referee Hugh Brown, added to our pantheon of Ayrshire village insults by declaring that East Ayrshire's Stewarton "is not twinned with anywhere else, but has an Asbo agreement with Cumnock."

"PRINCE William and Kate were confused when they visited the Emirates Stadium in Glasgow's east end yesterday," a reader phones to tell us. "They saw so many locals walking about in tracksuits they thought it was the opening ceremony of the Commonwealth Games they were attending."

BUCKS Fizz singer Cheryl Baker was on the telly talking about the eight hours she was stuck in her car because of the snow down south.

Someone who knows way too much about their Eurovision hit "Making Your Mind Up" tells us: "She of all people should know that to drive in snow you gotta speed it up, and then you gotta slow it down."

A SHOW about the late, great, Scottish folk singer Hamish Imlach is being performed at Rutherglen Town Hall. It reminds us of when Hamish and fellow folkie Josh Macrae were at Glasgow Airport to meet Soldier Blue singer Buffy Sainte-Marie, Ramblin' Jack Elliott, billed as "America's Roving Cowboy," and Blind Gary Davis, the black blues great, who were flying in for a folk festival. Naturally Hamish and Josh went for a few libations first.

At the terminal Hamish asked Josh: "How will we recognise them?" Josh replied: "A blind black man, a Cree Indian and a cowboy? If we don't recognise them, Hamish, I'm giving up drink."

TAGGART star Alex Norton was on a bus back into the centre of Edinburgh after attending Andrew Kinghorn's exhibition at the Sculpture Workshop when an inebriated chap got on, and greeted him with a "I've no seen you for ages! How's it gaun?" Alex gave a noncomittal "Oh fine – nice to see you too" reply as folk often think they know him.

But the chap persisted: "You dinnae remember me, dae ye? Dae ye no' recognise me?" And with that he whipped off his glasses and beamed at Alex, who beamed back: "Oh, of course! It's you! The specs . . ." At that the drunk was gratified, and the rest of the bus appreciated Alex's acting masterclass.

VETERAN Belfast punk band Stiff Little Fingers, fronted by Jake Burns, will be playing Glasgow's Barrowland on St Patrick's Day. Tony Gaughan tells us he was on the stage at Glasgow's Apollo before an appearance by the band and watched as a roadie put a yellow and black stripe at the front of the stage, which has a 20ft drop to the audience area, and then wrote "Stop!" in large letters.

When Tony asked why he was doing it, the roadie merely replied: "Jake. He's as blind as a bat."

THE Oscars saw Mark Andrews, director of Scottish-themed *Brave*, wear a kilt to collect his statuette, which had people wondering if this was the first Oscar-winning kilt wearer. We liked Mark's sense of humour when he was asked if *Brave* was the first animated Disney film with male nudity.

"No," replied Mark. "In *Ratatouille* they weren't wearing anything," referring of course to the film about Parisian rats.

AWARD-WINNING author Hilary Mantel has been criticised for apparently describing Kate Middleton as like a shop window mannequin with a plastic smile.

Our royal watcher tells us: "I'm not saying Kate's slow on the uptake, but when Prince William warned her not to look at the Mantel piece she spent the day avoiding fireplaces."

MUSIC fans are still talking about the great Bruce Springsteen concert at Hampden Park in Glasgow. Says Allan Boyd in Clarkston: "Bruce inadvertently became very Glaswegian when he asked sax player Jake Clemens to come forward to dance onstage with a fan during Dancing in the Dark. Bruce actually shouted out, 'Come on down, Jakey!'"

AS the sports pages are full of paeans to Sir Alex Ferguson, we remember instead the story of when he was a feisty young Rangers player unhappy at being dropped. He stormed into the hallowed manager's office at Ibrox and asked Scot Symon why he had been in the second team for three weeks.

"Because we don't have a third team," replied Symon.

FORMER US President Bill Clinton was making a point at the Scottish Business Awards, where he was guest speaker, about the level of surveillance in our lives by explaining how everyone now has camera phones.

So he asked the question: "Do you know the difference between when I played golf at St Andrews today and when I played there 10 years ago?" He perhaps wasn't expecting the Scottish businessman who shouted out: "10 shots?"

A READER in London was in his local where a couple of topers were discussing Billy Connolly still performing at the age of 70. "And don't forget," one of them added, "it's even more impressive when you realise that's 280 in Glasgow years."

THE GLASTONBURY Festival was on at the weekend, and the set by the Rolling Stones which was televised on Saturday night showed the band members are no longer in their first flush of youth. As Tom Jamieson comments: "The band's backstage demands were that the Government doesn't scrap the winter fuel allowance for wealthy pensioners."

And someone not a fan of outdoor festivals tells us: "Recreate the Glastonbury experience by playing the Rolling Stones in your kitchen, and listening from a puddle two streets away."

CROONER Robbie Williams held his second sell-out concert at Glasgow's Hampden Park last night. Not everyone though is a fan. As one reader phoned to tell us: "I feel sorry for folk who live near Hampden – having to keep their windows closed on what was such a lovely evening."

AS the stories of 1970s television personalities being interviewed by the police continue, Jimmy Manson in Ayr reveals to us: "At golf this morning somebody said, 'Have you heard any good Jimmy Tarbuck jokes yet?' "I said, 'I didn't know he told any.'"

CELEBRITY stories. Graham Scott, retired journalist, says: "After a concert at the Glasgow Apollo, I had time to relax with Ted

Nugent, 'the world's loudest guitar player', over drinks in the lobby of the also long gone Albany Hotel.

"The young lady perched on his lap decided to wear his stetson and was told: 'Careful honey, that's my lucky hat.' 'How's it cried yer lucky hat?', she asked. Ted told her: 'Just keep wearing it honey, you'll find out.'"

SCOTTISH author Irvine Welsh was one of many Scots watching Andy Murray at Wimbledon.

We think he might be stretching the truth a little when he declares: "Wimbledon facts – since they opened up the ball boy's role to non-orphans, the number of fatalities through beatings by umpires has fallen 86%."

THE acclaimed National Theatre play Black Watch, about disillusioned Scots soldiers, is on at the SECC from March 28 after playing around the world. At one point in the production the soldiers joke about who would play them in a film, with one of them told, much to his annoyance, that for him they would need "the b****** who played the Elephant Man".

The cast still have a card that was sent to them by John Hurt after a previous performance which reads: "Loved the show," signed by, "The b****** who played the Elephant Man."

COATBRIDGE writer Andy Bollen, who was drummer in a group that supported the band Nirvana, has revealed the shocking news in his just published book Nirvana A Tour Diary that singer Kurt Cobain and his wife Courtney Love were Bay City Rollers fans.

Andy tells us: "We were on tour in Sheffield and I was standing at a market stall, going through records, when Kurt sidled up to a box next to me for a chat and pulled out a Bay City Rollers album and revealed his love for them. I suppose it could have been worse, it might have been Lulu."

EVEN that august newspaper the *Wall Street Journal* can make mistakes. A reader sends us a cutting of a correction which states: "Talking about performing in the musical *The Who's Tommy*, the actor and singer Michael Cerveris said: 'I couldn't sing it all when I got the job.

"Our article incorrectly quoted him as saying: 'I couldn't sing at all when I got the job.'"

THE BBC is celebrating the 200th edition of its short celebrity interview programme, Five Minutes With. We remember the reply by comedian Ed Byrne, who got into the business by running comedy nights in his local pub in Glasgow, when he was asked on the programme: "In a nutshell, how did you become a comedian?" Replied Ed: "I didn't do it in a nutshell. It's very hard to perform comedy in a nutshell. Atmosphere is very important. I find theatres to be far better places to do it."

ACCORDIONIST Phil Cunningham admitted at the opening concert of Celtic Connections, now under way in Glasgow, that he played before the Queen at Balmoral, and afterwards Her Majesty asked him how difficult it was to co-ordinate his hands while playing the accordion. Cunningham said he feels like an idiot when he recalls his reply: "Have you ever patted your head and rubbed your stomach at the same time?"

BBC presenter Kaye Adams, compering the Scottish Law Awards, admitted she is still having problems with Twitter. She was on a train from Partick at 7am when she watched the unusual breakfast arrangements of the young girl opposite and tweeted: "Girl opposite me having a Crunchie and Red Bull for breakfast. Waiting for her eyes to pop and her head to turn 360 degrees."

At Coatbridge Sunnyside the girl got up to leave, tapped Kaye on the shoulder, and said: "It wisnae a Crunchie – it was a Wispa Gold."

5
Students

From present-day students, back to getting the belt at school, education really is a laughing matter.

A STUDENT who had just moved into halls of residence in Glasgow was walking along Maryhill Road when a rough-looking chap asked him if he could spare a fag. "I don't smoke," replied the student. "So you're not fae Maryhill then?" the chap opined.

ST ANDREWS University is often accused of not having enough native students. One of the Scottish students tells us: "I heard a posh English student tell his pal the problem with his new girlfriend was that she could only speak a few words of English. He then added, 'But on the plus side, Dundee girls are such great fun.'"

WE OFTEN remark on the strange conversations folk hear on buses. A Shawlands reader said he was going to work yesterday when a teenage girl told her pal: "We had scrambled eggs for breakfast, but it was like a pancake." Her pal thought about this before replying: "You mean an omelette?"

OUR FIRE ALARM picture reminded Jean Miller of a friend who was a fire prevention officer, visiting a Cambuslang school which had a new alarm system installed. He told the head teacher that she could activate it by hitting it with the heel of her shoe.

Now the head teacher was obviously an intelligent woman as she wouldn't have become a head teacher otherwise, but she did nonetheless reply: "How do I get my leg up to that height?"

IT WAS 30 years ago that the pound coin was introduced in Britain.

We remember the tale of the Aberdonian chemistry teacher who took a pound coin out of his pocket, poured sulphuric acid over it, and asked if it would dissolve.

"No," said one of the class. "Good," said the teacher, "And why not?" "If it did, you'd have used a penny," said the pupil.

OUR MENTION of Italian surnames reminds Paul Cortopassi in Bonnybridge: "I'm still not sure if a former pupil was really confused or just taking the mickey when he headed an exam paper for the attention of Mr Cort O'Passi. At least my Irish grandmother would have enjoyed the joke."

A WEST-END reader admits to divining a certain logic when he overheard a student-type on his mobile phone on Glasgow's Byres Road explaining: "I know money doesn't grow on trees mum. That's why I'm asking you for some."

CARDONALD COLLEGE is to merge with Anniesland and Langside colleges this summer to form Glasgow Clyde College. We've always been impressed by its students, but we recall when the great Glasgow students' charity magazine *Ygorra* made reference to a student "who was so stupid he would have difficulty obtaining entrance to Cardonald College".

It was claimed the college principal complained and was given the retraction "*Ygorra* accepts that no student is so stupid that he or she would be refused admission to Cardonald College."

MORE FROM student charities mag *Ygorra*, as Tom Bain in Uddingston told us: "Much intellectual effort was focused on devising a suitable slogan with which to browbeat ambushed Glaswegians into contributing to Charities Week.

"Two examples were Squaw Shinabob (younger readers may have to have 'bob' explained to them) and Phil McCann."

WE ASKED for your memories of *Ygorra*, and Enid Reid happily remembered being allowed to travel on Glasgow buses for free during charity week in the early seventies so that you could politely harass the passengers for contributions.

Others, though, just wanted to sneak in jokes once published by the magazine, such as the reader who told us: "Last night I was in a car crash. My car hit the wall between two family homes. In one house lived the Balls and in the other lived the Whites. Thank goodness I was pulled out by the Whites."

JIM McDONALD dug out an old copy of *Ygorra* from the 1980s which included a conversation between two Russian soldiers.

"Morning Vladimir."
"Morning Ivan."
"Chilly today."
"No we've not finished with Afghanistan yet."

IT'S TOUGH trying to help schoolchildren with their homework. A Glasgow father tells us: "Helping my son with his English, I explained to him what an oxymoron was. When I asked if it made sense, he replied, 'Clear as mud.'"

WE MENTIONED university exam questions, and Chic Duncan tells us that when he was studying philosophy at Glasgow University in the 1980s one exam question was simply "Why?" It was claimed that the student who merely answered "Why not?" was given a pass mark.

OUR REQUEST for school belt tales has stung you into action. One reader recalls: "I was at school in Rutherglen where a nice young lady teacher regularly lost control. We were visited by her male colleague from next door who selected random innocent bystanders and belted them.

"On complaining, I was advised – and I have remembered it to this day – "no-one ever said anything in life is fair.""

MORE BELT stories as a former teacher tells us of an occasion when he was a student teacher in the East End of Glasgow in the 1970s, and the PE head stopped a playground rammy. "The miscreants were lined up in the playground, and the belt was used along the line until reaching one vociferously protesting youth.

"There were to be no arguments though, and he was duly belted and dismissed. It was only established later, after a call from the bread company, that the protesting youth was in fact the apprentice van boy who was delivering rolls to the dinner school."

ALAN BARLOW in Paisley says: "Our English teacher used to belt the class in alphabetical order for failing to learn poetry. My first place was finally taken when a boy called Anderson joined the class. As he was a six-footer with a build to match he took the sting out of the punishment for the rest of us.

"There was an obvious disadvantage in having the initials AB in class situations, and I used to insist that my real surname was Zimmerman – which now describes me perfectly."

OUR SCHOOL belt stories show how times have changed. Helen Wilson remembers being in a misbehaving primary seven class in the 1960s whose teacher declared they were all going to be belted.

As he didn't want to spend the time belting them all, he brought them forward in pairs and got them to belt each other.

"I can't begin to imagine the furore, should such a thing happen these days," says Helen.

JOHN ROBERTSON tells us about his pal talking in class and the maths teacher shouting: "Do you want the belt boy?" Says John: "My mate replied 'No'. 'No what?' he barked back at him, expecting him to say 'No sir'. My mate replied, 'No thanks'. Obviously the belt then made an appearance."

TIME to tuck our school belting stories up the sleeve of our cloak, but not before Alex Moir in Ayr passes on: "In Cranhill Secondary in the early 1960s our English teacher did not like to belt girls, so he paired each girl with a boy in his class.

"If the boy misbehaved he was belted, and if the girl misbehaved the boy paired with her was belted.

"Can you imagine that happening today?"

YES, we finished our school belt stories, but there's a late addition from Morton Dewar: "My history master at Edinburgh Academy was fond of asking pupils to write short notes on well-known historical characters.

"One day he posed the question, 'Who was Pericles?' In an inspired moment I wrote that: Pericles was a brother of Testicles. The ensuing tawsing ensured that I have never had an inspired moment since."

OUR MENTION of learning foreign languages reminds David Donaldson: "A friend who earned his crust teaching art at a fairly rough school in Glasgow tells fondly of the day the new German student teacher arrived at the school gates with his blond hair in a distinctly Teutonic short style.

"By the morning break, every pupil in the playground knew him as Herr Kutt."

ANDY MURRAY'S big week at Wimbledon reminded us of the student at Glasgow Yoonie who confided: "Mortified to discover my mates only call me the Love Machine because I'm rubbish at tennis."

THE UNIVERSITY of St Andrews has always had a reputation for attracting posh students. So a Glasgow father in the town for his daughter's graduation ceremony couldn't believe it when he saw a sign at the car park for the university's Bute Building which states: "Four spaces reserved for Bentleys."

He tells us: "I was ranting about it later to some local lads in a St Andrews pub, going on and on about how the rich shouldn't be given such privileges. When I eventually took a breath, one of the locals told me, 'The hall's being renovated by a Dundee firm of shopfitters, Bentleys. The spaces are for their vans.'"

OUR TALE about whether Jim Apple would struggle giving his name in France reminds Allan Boyd in Glasgow of a modern languages teacher friend who kicked off a test with the relatively simple name enquiry: "Comment t'appelles tu?" She felt one chap who was going to struggle was the one who looked at her and replied: "Aye, you've got me there, miss."

A BEARSDEN reader tells us her 17-year-old daughter is learning to drive and offered to take her parents to church on Sunday. When they arrived the teenage girl's dad said: "thank you."

When their daughter said he didn't have to thank her, he replied: "I was talking to God."

TALKING of odd names, Ken Wimbor reveals: "My wife, a teacher, recently came across a girl with the forward-looking name of Tamara Knight."

AS UNIVERSITIES wind down for the end of term, a reader in Glasgow's west end heard one student coming out of the library telling his pal: "I'm finished with learning anything new unless they can prove to me that Google won't exist in the future."

AYSHIRE TEACHER George Crawford tells us they had a Book and Bake event at school to raise money for Yorkhill Children's Hospital which involved reading books while enjoying some cake.

The eating and reading led to some appropriate book titles being suggested for the event, including: *Anne of Green Bagels*; *The Buns of Navarone*; *Gateau on a Hot Tin Roof* and of course, *The Life of Pie*.

WE MENTIONED appropriate book titles after Largs Academy held a charity read-a-book-and-eat-cake event. School librarian Theresa Newbury says she has been inundated with requests for: *Tess of the Caramels*; *One Flew Over The Meringue Nest*; *The Pie Who Came In From The Cold*; *Cake Expectations*.

DAVID DONALDSON suggests: *Scone With The Wind*; *Swiss Family Roll And Son*; *Tom Brownie's Schooldays*; and the inspired *The Chouxmakers Wife*.

WE TURN the gas off on our book titles to complement baking with Stephen Gold suggesting: *Batch 22*; *War and Piece* and of course for *Star Wars* fans, *The Empire Biscuit Strikes Back*.

ANOTHER DAD who thinks he's a comedian. A young Bothwell girl doing her homework asked her dad what a chameleon looked like. "Here, I'll draw one for you." Two minutes later he handed her back a blank sheet of paper.

OUR JOB vacancy story reminds David Macleod in Lenzie: "I remember seeing a hotel job advertised which, as well as a generous salary, offered a 'sleeping-in allowance'. Great job for a student, I thought."

A PIECE of whimsy from a computer savvy reader who tells us: "Of course my password's insecure. So would you be if you were replaced every six months."

DADS who think they are funny, continued. A student from Rutherglen phoned her parents from university in Manchester, and after chatting to her dad, asked: "So is mum handy?" "Oh yes," replied dad. "She's finished making my dinner and has started on some sewing."

A TEACHER desperate for the summer break swears to us he asked his class what the difference was between ignorance and apathy. A pupil replied: "Don't know and don't care."

AS THE SCHOOL year draws to a close, a teacher in the West End, who works in one of the city's more challenging schools, tells us she was taking the details of a new pupil and asked him his father's name.

The little one replied that his father was away, but his mum's new boyfriend stayed with them.

Teacher asked for the boyfriend's name, and when the boy told her, another voice piped up from the class: "I had him last year. He's rubbish."

ANOTHER teacher begging for the school year to end is the one who pointed out to his primary class pupil that 18 plus 18 in his jotter was 36, and not 32. "When did that change?" the youngster asked him.

OUR TALE of schoolchildren teasing the lollipop man reminds Alan Frame of his schooldays: "Flagging down an approaching bus, we would wait innocently until the driver stopped and opened the doors for us to climb aboard. Instead, we would place a foot on the platform, quickly tie our shoelace and then politely thank the driver before walking off.

"We discovered some hitherto unheard nuances of the English language, which was really quite educational and enlightening."

A TEACHER'S tale on our school belt stories. Says Angela Simms: "As a young French teacher in Possilpark in the 1970s I rarely gave the belt, but one day I had threatened the 33 boys in 3F4 four times with the belt if they didn't stop talking.

"As they laughed, I had to keep my word. The next day, my last before maternity leave, one of them put a lovely pram quilt on my desk and said, 'Miss that's for your wean – will ye bring it in tae see us?' Feeling really bad, I was consoled by an older, cynical, male colleague, who said, 'Don't worry – they probably knocked it from that wee baby shop in Saracen Street.'"

FRANK O'DONNELL tells us about his secondary school in Glasgow in the 1970s where one of the teachers was called Mr McHugh. Whenever he had to dish out the belt to a number of miscreants he would regularly chant: "Form a queue for Mr McHugh."

OUR SCHOOL belt stories bring back painful memories for Alan Stewart in Prestwick, who tells us: "When I was a teenager I was 'awarded' two of the belt for forgetting a book, and I ended up with severe bruising on my right wrist.

"When I returned home I showed my wrist to my mother, in the hope of receiving some maternal sympathy.

"When she asked me why I got the belt, and I told her, I then got a skelp on the ear and told, 'Well you won't forget it again then will you?'"

A FINAL school belt story as Cecilia Murray tells us of being a teacher in Glasgow and helping out with the Christmas production of *Cinderella*.

Says Cecilia: "The three children acting as the mice for Cinderella's coach were being unruly backstage. To restore order a male teacher belted the mice, in their magnificent mice costumes.

"Could you imagine that being filmed on mobile phones nowadays?"

NEWS from the University of St Andrews where student journalist Jamie Ross stood to become president of the Students' Association with the slogan: "Student elections are pointless," promising he would spend his election budget on shoes. And he failed to attend the hustings meeting as he had an expiring yoghurt.

Guess what. He got nearly 1,000 votes – more than any other candidate – but was later eliminated on the transferrable vote system.

We think he might have a future in politics.

INCIDENTALLY, Jamie stated that he was fed up with posh St Andrews students making fun of the locals. To see if he had a point we checked the students' website where Cara Nikita Bancroft writes: "Saw a girl who looked really young on South Street pushing a pram who told her friend, 'I would have liked to have been older when I had her. Sixteen would have been nice.'"

IT MAY come as a bit of a shock to some parents of teenagers, but they are known to sometimes carry a fake ID with them in order to get into licensed premises.

One chap who failed at a Glasgow pub at the weekend was the youngster who was stopped at the door and asked for identification. Perhaps he had already been drinking as, momentarily confused, he reached into his pocket and asked the doorman: "Which one is it? The 21 or the 18-year-old?"

A LENZIE reader says she took her car to the garage to be checked over as there was a strange whining noise coming from it when she was driving. "Has your daughter left her One Direction CD playing?" the mechanic asked her.

A WEST-of-Scotland drama teacher tells us she was discussing with a class the ability of some actors to cry when it suits them. The teacher explained: "They think of something that usually makes them cry. Try it yourselves."

She then asked the class after a couple of minutes what they had been thinking about, and one non-crying girl replied: "Onions."

OUR MENTION of fake IDs to get into bars reminds a barman in a Glasgow club of the time the premises offered a free drink to anyone on their birthday.

When one chap came up to claim it, the barman pointed out he needed to see something with his date of birth on it.

The chap pulled out his student card and the barman read it and told him: "Yes, it is your birthday – but unfortunately you're 17 today," and had to send him packing.

WE ASKED for your stories of Glasgow student magazine *Ygorra*, and Yvonne Neville recalls a different era and tells us: "*Ygorra* in the 1950s had a cartoon of a frazzled prim teacher standing in front of a class of eager five-year-olds, telling them, 'The curriculum requires me to teach you about sex and other filthy stuff.'"

A READER tells us his teenage daughter was getting exasperated at her parents questioning her about her preparation for her upcoming school exams. "You sound like the Spanish Armada!" she shouted at them. "So not going to do so well in history," thought her dad.

OUR MENTION of *Ygorra* and the Glasgow students' charity week slogans reminds George Wishart in Dumfries and Galloway: "There was Krama Khan Fu (Mongolian influence), Caesyer Cash (Roman influence), Poohshyerbitin (A. A. Milne influence) and B Jenny Russ (Probably under the influence)."

THANKS to many for recalling the punning characters who fronted rag week in Glasgow over the years, including the Bedouin-style Sheik Yapokits, the dashing Sir Ender Ramunny, the sultry Doneta Peseta, the dinosaur Anditaur, the Russian Hannah Bobova, Butcher Cashin, and Geisha Yen Hen.

If you can't work any of those names out, ask a Glaswegian over the age of 50.

A LANARKSHIRE reader's teenage son announced he was con-templating joining the army when he left school. While his two older brothers ripped into him about how useless he would be either with a rifle or in close combat, the most devastating riposte came from his mother, who asked: "Do you really plan to make your own bed every morning?"

NOSTALGIA alert. Our tales of excuses for being late remind Alan Morrison of queuing up overnight at a Glasgow record store with his school-chum for tickets to see the Rolling Stones many years ago. Unfortunately they were so late for school in Govan the next day that they were given six of the belt. The teacher added that they looked as if they had been sleeping outside. When they said they had, they got another six of the belt for being cheeky.

Later that day, a picture of them in the front of the queue for the Stones tickets was in the *Evening Times*, thus confirming their tale. "That's 12 I owe you," was the teacher's response.

6
Shopping

Some people were shocked at the horsemeat scandal. *Herald* **readers just laughed.**

DAFT GAG of the weekend? The woman who went into the Glasgow furniture store and asked: "Is that an occasional table?" "Naw," replied the young assistant, "it's always a table."

NATURALLY readers were snorting at the horsemeat found in supermarket burgers news story. One reader swore to us: "I saw a wee old man leaving Tesco at Silverburn with a bottle of Bacardi and a packet of burgers. 'Is that white rum and Red Rum?' I asked him.

And John Day in Houston claimed: "Apparently they are going to be rebranded as My Lidl Pony."

SLIGHTLY more subtle was Michael Walton who told us: "I've just checked the burgers in our freezer . . . and they're off!"

SADLY fruit is still a foreign land to many Scots. Dominic Gribben in Ardrossan tells us: "At the supermarket checkout I was served by a young man who looked at the yellow fruit I had bought, then at the list of fruits on his screen, and asked: "Ur they lemons?" "No," I replied, "they're grapefruit."

The chap looked puzzled before replying: "Naw, they're the wee green yins."

A PARTICULARLY crafty piece of advertising in the window of Crocket the Ironmonger in Glasgow. Amid the wellies, the midge repellent and the wind-up lanterns, we spotted a small tub containing a handful of fly swats, £1.50 each.

Fly swats are fly swats, but Crocket managed to come up with a line that makes you smile. It read: "Andy Murray started with these."

YOU'LL remember the story about a Sainsbury's check-out assistant refusing to serve a customer who was talking on her mobile phone.

Fair enough, you might have thought. But the boot is sometimes on the other foot. From Wishaw we hear of a grandfatherly type in a supermarket with a trolleyful of groceries who failed to get a greeting from the check-out girl.

Not a word was spoken as she scanned the items. When he asked how much he was due, she merely pointed to the till display. Still silence reigned. Transaction complete, our friend decided to remind her about common courtesy.

"Does anyone say thanks any more?" he asked.

At which the girl uttered her only words: "It's written on your ticket."

BOUGHT a computer recently? A reader muses: "Nestle should follow Apple's example and create the After Nine which would be slightly taller and slightly thinner than the After Eight."

WE MENTIONED the Coca Cola bottles with names on them and a reader swears that he heard a young chap ask his father if he could search the Coke bottles for his name, and his father replied: "Why don't you have a Pepsi, Max?"

A READER was in his local shop when the pensioner in front of him handed over a basket of groceries which came to more than eight quid.

"I can't afford that on my pension," declared the old lady, who instructed the shop assistant not to ring up the cauliflower in the basket.

Our reader was just about to offer to pay for the vegetable when the old dear then told the assistant: "And two scratchcards."

A READER in Glasgow's city centre on Sunday watched a woman cross Argyle Street with what appeared to be her husband following a couple of desultory steps behind.

He assumed it was her husband as the chap was shouting at the back of the woman, who was giving no indication that she was listening: "Why did my wife cross the road? To get to the blinkin' shop we first went into an hour ago."

A WEST-END reader swears he heard a teenager tell his pal that he saw a tarantula spider on sale in a pet shop for forty quid. His pal replied: "You'd get it cheaper off the web."

DONALD RITCHIE in Gourock was in a supermarket which was selling leggings under a large label stating: "Ladies bottoms". A female shopper remarked: "If I knew they were selling them I'd have bought a smaller one."

THE FRENCH TENNIS Open, or Roland Garros Tournament as it is known in France, has an online store where you can buy fashion items.

Reader Jim Graham was bemused to discover that many items are named after Scottish towns – there is a Clydebank skirt, a Bellshill T-shirt, an Alloway hoodie and a Beith T-shirt.

Well done the French for still supporting the entente cordiale, although it would surely be somewhat churlish to suggest that few men in Bellshill or Beith sporting a T-shirt could be mistaken for a French tennis star.

SHOPPING at his local greengrocer's the other day a reader heard another shopper complain to the owner that the iceberg lettuces seemed small. "The icebergs? It's global warming," the chap rather wittily replied.

MILKMAN Tom Barr in Prestwick is still puzzling over the call he got from a woman who told him: "My neighbour must have forgotten to cancel her milk before she died yesterday."

A READER tells us he and his wife visited the Renfrew branch of retail chain B&Q where his wife asked the helpful chap at the door where the toilet was.

"Are ye burstin'?" he asked, a question not put to the customer since she was at school.

It turned out he was not obsessed with matters urological but was helpfully suggesting there was a disabled toilet nearby if it was a pressing matter rather than having to stroll to the far end of the store.

OUR TALES of red wine reminds Graham Shaw in Kirkcudbright of the classic line of the lady at Glasgow Airport reporting that her suitcase had not arrived. The chap taking her complaint asked what colour it was and she replied: "Wine."

"Red or white?" he enquired.

"I BOUGHT a self-help CD entitled *How to Handle Disappointment*," said the chap in the Glasgow pub at the weekend. "When I got home and opened it, I found the box was empty."

AND NOW Blockbuster in administration. Although many readers had not been there for years – which explains its financial difficulties – one reminisced: "Do you remember hiring a film on a Friday night then getting up early on Saturday to watch it again before you had to return it?"

A SHAWLANDS reader shopping in the supermarket was queuing behind an old chap who was studying the leaflets for various financial services on offer by the company. The old chap turned to our reader and declared: "Do I want a mortgage? Just how much is this trolley of messages going to be?"

DAFT GAG of the week? The chap who announced: "I was ordering some goods online and stupidly used my donor card instead of my credit card when giving my details. It ended up costing me an arm and a leg."

A GLASGOW reader swears to us he was in his local corner shop when a chap came in with a dog on a lead and the shop owner told him: "Sorry. No dogs." The chap merely replied: "I didn't think you would have any. It's actually a Mars Bar I'm looking for."

IT CAN be embarrassing taking your bored husband shopping with you. A reader heard one such chap observe rather too loudly in a Glasgow department store: "I know the girls on the make-up counters get free samples. But surely they don't have to use them all at once?"

A READER tells us he was in a Maryhill supermarket behind a young chap who was buying a pile of paper plates and disposable knives and forks.

The chatty person on the till asked the customer: "Having a party?"

"No," replied the customer. But as the cashier continued to look quizzical, the customer added: "I just can't be bothered washing dishes."

WE'VE MENTIONED before the amusing reviews left on the internet shopping site Amazon when anyone buys the products they sell. A reader points us to the latest review for bottles of Barrettine methylated spirit, which may sound rather a mundane product. However the latest review states: "From the moment you remove the cap you realise you're in for a treat. Fresh, bright, smoky, with a mineral edge and rounded, fruity nose.

"Bold, possessing some edge and no little bite, yet remaining smooth, balanced and satisfying. This is a drink to enjoy with friends in a park. Highly recommended."

TALKING of the west end, a reader was in an upmarket super-market there when a woman remonstrated with her young son who wasn't behaving himself by telling him: "Be good – or I'll buy extra broccoli."

CHRISTMAS present buying is in full swing, and a shifty-looking character in a Glasgow pub was heard explaining: "I got the kids a trampoline from the internet." "What website did you see it on?" asked his mate. "Google Earth," he replied.

BILL THOMPSON in Lenzie was in the Marks and Spencer store in Sauchiehall Street when he read a sign on the wall stating "Cash machine available in womenswear." He thought to himself: "That's very chic" and wondered how often they changed its outfit.

READER Davie Adams was seeking religious-themed postage stamps for his Christmas cards rather than the red-nosed reindeer ones more readily available. Says Davie: "The assistant in one Post

Office told me he had offered a woman either reindeer or Madonna and Child stamps. 'Aw, gie us Rudolf,' she replied, 'Ah cannae staun' that Madonna wumman, takin' thae weans away frae Africa.'"

SOME of you poor souls will be gearing up for the sales. A Glasgow shop assistant tells us that a customer came in after last Christmas seeking a refund, and our reader had to explain this was only possible with the receipt. But the customer explained that it was a present.

"Can you not get the receipt from the person who bought it? Who gave you the present?" asked our man.

"Santa," replied the customer.

BUSINESS NEWS, and we learn that Trevor Moore, the chief executive of HMV when it went into administration, was originally headhunted from Jessops, the camera store which also put the shutters up this week, as it were. "Did he start off as safety officer on the Titanic?" a reader asks.

"I GOT an Amazon voucher for Christmas," announced the Glasgow chap in the pub the other night. "I've ordered two piranha fish and a pygmy."

OUR APPRENTICE stories remind David Yule: "At East Kilbride police station in the 1980s, sending a probationer out in the middle of the night armed with a wee step ladder, a bucket of water and a shammy to polish the Belisha beacons on the zebra crossings was common.

"Many a citizen returning home in the wee sma' hours must have been intrigued to see a young police officer up a step ladder washing them while just up the street would be a patrol car full of sniggering older coppers."

7
Tuck In

Quite a few laughs are served up when Scots go out to eat.

A GLASGOW reader hears a chap in his local pub tell about taking his kids to a fast food restaurant at the weekend where the table was covered in so much debris from previous meals that he had to spend a good five minutes clearing it up before they could eat.

"Did the staff thank you?" asked one of his mates.

"Thank me?" the chap replied. "My picture's up on the wall as employee of the month."

TOM HOSIE was in a west-end restaurant when a couple complained the dessert they had ordered was taking a long time to arrive.

Says Tom: "The dessert duly arrived, and a short time later, in no doubt an attempt to placate further, the manager stopped at their table and asked whether the couple were celebrating anything special.

"'Just the arrival of the dessert,'" was the reply.

DAFT GAG for the weekend? The chap who made dinner for his new girlfriend and told her: "Those chips you've just eaten actually came from my garden this morning."

"Wow," she smiled, "I didn't know you grew potatoes."

"I don't," the chap told her. "Some drunk must have thrown them over the hedge last night."

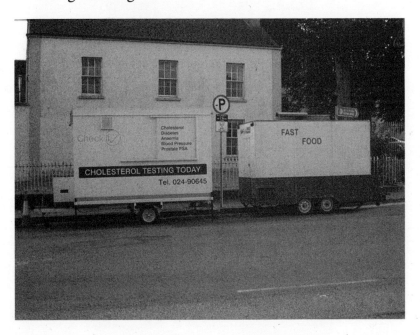

SCOTTISH dining habits can sometimes seem unique. John Newlands was in a fashionable Italian restaurant in St Andrews when the waiter asked the Fife wifey at the next table, while he proffered a dish of grated cheese: "Parmesan?" "Just oan ma chips please," the lady replied.

A READER phones: "I walked into Burger King and asked for a Whopper. 'Certainly sir', said the assistant. 'Our burgers contain no horse meat.'"

AND the gags continue. Says Graham Richmond: "I was at the doctor for a check-up, and he told me I should try to watch what I eat. So I've bought two tickets for Ayr races."

MIKE RITCHIE was in a hotel, which is now closed, funnily enough in Angus, where an American diner complained to the waiter that his steak was tough and the vegetables undercooked. "Nothing like speaking your mind is there, sir?" said the waitress, before walking away.

DINING OUT continued. Jim Hair in Dalry was in a now-former hotel where a large party of diners were fobbed off by the waiting staff when they wanted to complain about the quality of the food.

When they eventually found the manager he told them: "You've come to the right person – because I couldn't care either."
Adds Jim: "The hotel later closed, burned down, and is now a street of lovely houses."

KIRSTY BUCHANAN tells us of a friend's family dining in an American-themed restaurant in Glasgow where an enthusiastic waitress with an American accent took their order. Says Kirsty: "After she left my friend was wondering aloud whether or not she was really an American or if it was just an act to keep the theme running.

"Her brother was quick to respond with some authority, 'with a name like Trainee she's bound to be American.'"

OUR STORY of waiters and their names reminds Andrew Haddow of the time he was dining with his brother and his brother's then girlfriend when the waiter came over and announced: "Hi, I'll be your waiter today, and I'm Randy." Says Andrew: "My brother and I didn't dare look at each other for some time."

RESTAURANT group Zizzi has opened a diner in the former Borders bookstore in Glasgow's Royal Exchange Square. It has been given a phone number which is only one digit away from that of the Western Infirmary, which has led to a number of wrong calls. Events manager Andrew Stewart swears a chap phoned about being booked in, and a member of staff asked if it was a table for two.

After a lengthy pause, the caller said he didn't think things were so bad that he would have to share an operating table to have his haemorrhoids seen to.

WE DO wonder how foreigners cope with Scotland at times. A Kilmarnock reader was having lunch in a local restaurant when his wife asked for cream with her sticky toffee pudding. "Pouring or skooshy?" asked the waitress.

A YOUNG waitress at a Glasgow burger joint is pleading for her customers to come up with some new patter. She says whenever she asks customers if they want anything on their burger, she wants them to know that they are not the first to tell her: "Five pounds each way."

OUR TALES of ordering wine remind Tony Sykes: "In a friendly wee pub in Dumfries I had to advise the waitress I had ordered a bottle of the 1977 but she had brought me the 1978. With impeccable logic she said, 'Well it will be fresher then.'"

ORDERING WINE continued. Says Tim Huntingford: "In a Campbeltown restaurant, I ordered a bottle of French red wine which was number 15 on the wine list. The waitress arrived with the bottle, but it was white and Italian. When I queried this, she explained that they hadn't any left of number 15, so she had brought number 16 instead.

"Too stunned to question this impeccable logic, we drank the white without complaint."

SKY SPORTS NEWS has asked viewers to suggest the name of a racehorse they are going to sponsor. One of the first suggestions is Mincemeat with the viewer saying: "Because it would make mincemeat of the opposition." We don't think that's really the reason he suggested it.

OUR dining tale reminds Craig Bradshaw: "My dad went to a posh hotel in Belfast for dinner where the waitress took his order, which included a starter of prawns Marie Rose.

"Ten minutes later she apologetically reappeared and asked him if he'd like to change his order to prawns Marie Celeste – as the kitchen had run out of prawns."

IN the west end the other week when the weather was roasting a reader was supermarket shopping and heard two young people discussing whether to buy a bag of ice for a party they were having later in their back garden.

"It will melt before we get it home," one of them said.

"If it does, we can put it in the freezer," the other replied.

AUTHOR Deedee Cuddihy was posting a birthday gift to her grand-daughter in Brussels when the Post Office assistant handed out a leaflet on items banned from international mail. The chap behind her took a copy and read out: "Vodka, whisky, ammunition, cannabis, cocaine, fireworks, flares, flick knives and pepper spray. Where I come from that's got the makings of a right good party."

BARBECUES have been all the rage the past few weeks, but it has meant a few chaps having to meet their neighbours for the first time socially. We are told of one such gathering in Bishopbriggs where a chap collecting his burger asked a neighbour he didn't know: "So what do you do?" "Oh I've got a finger in a few pies," the neighbour bumptiously declared.

"So you're banned from Greggs then?" our burger-eater replied before his wife dragged him away.

UPMARKET supermarket Waitrose was bombarded with joke messages claiming it was pretentious after asking folk on Twitter to say why they shopped there. The messages remind Nigel Robson in Edinburgh of the boy in the private school uniform overheard asking his dad in Waitrose: "Does Lego have a 't' at the end like Merlot?"

A READER in a city-centre sandwich shop was behind a young girl who had a stack of about a dozen sandwiches which she was buying – presumably sent out on behalf of her colleagues at work.

As the large pile of cardboard boxes cascaded on to the counter, the bored assistant automatically asked: "Sitting in or taking away?"

"How fat do you think I am?" the young girl immediately replied.

8
You've Had One Too Many

Scots love a good night out, and if there is a laugh at the end of it, so much the better.

FOLK are girding up for the office Christmas parties. One ageing boss admitted to us that he was persuaded by younger staff to attend a trendy nightspot afterwards where the doorman stopped him and said: "Sorry bud. You've had too many."

"What, drinks?" asked the boss.

"No, birthdays," said the steward.

THE HILTON Hotel in Glasgow's city centre had a birthday bash to celebrate its 20 years in Glasgow with guests being entertained by local nine-piece soul band Counselled Out.

Lead vocalist Drew Robertson broke off from introducing the next number to tell his audience in the hotel foyer: "Please refrain from taking pictures of the band for security reasons."

A few folk nodded their heads in sympathy with the added

problems that life brings these days, when Drew added, after looking at his fellow band members: "Social security reasons."

PETE BECKLEY, named Reading Comedy Festival's New Act
of 2012, worked in IT until he signed up for a comedy course in
Edinburgh which he hoped would help him with his presentational
skills. Says Pete: "On the second lesson the comedy tutor asked us
all to get up and speak for five minutes. I was afraid the other people
there might laugh at me but the tutor assured me they wouldn't."

WE ASKED for your Glasgow Odeon stories before it's demol-
ished, and Alastair McSporran in Ross-shire recalls when Johnny
Cash appeared there in the late sixties, accompanied by his wife
June Carter. Says Alastair: "Towards the end of the show, June
chatted with the audience, and got a shouted response from three
US servicemen.
   "She asked them where they came from, and one by one they
shouted out their hometown.
   "The transatlantic twangs were interrupted by a gruff voice: 'An'
Ah'm fae Govan an' Ah've got a bus tae catch, so get a move on.'"

JIM THOMSON recalls: "I remember being serenaded by a
visually-impaired busker slowly making his way along the Odeon
queue. He was followed some paces behind by a down-at-heel guy
with cap in hand who, before he reached the head of the queue, did
a bunk with the collection."

WE ASKED for your Glasgow Odeon stories before it was demol-
ished, and Hilary Iannotti confesses: "Many years ago I met a boy

at a south-side disco who invited me to go to the pictures. I duly met him in Central Station and walked up to the Odeon. We sat near the back and I was praying I didn't meet anyone I knew as I couldn't believe I had agreed to go to the pictures with him.

"Just before the movie started I excused myself to go to the ladies, and sprinted to Glasgow Central to catch a train home. I do wonder if he was traumatised by the experience."

LATEST CINEMA favourite is the unfathomably successful *Twilight* film. As one cinema-goer told us: "I went to see *Twilight*, but it was ruined by some annoying girl talking the whole way through. Kristen Stewart I think her name was."

DODGY subtitling on the telly, and Ronnie MacQuarrie tells us his favourite was a report on childbirth which stated on the screen in some cases babies had to be delivered "by four Serbs".

DAFT gag of the week from a TV fan. "How many *Countdown* contestants does it take to change a BLIHBULGT?"

A POSTSCRIPT to the Edinburgh Fringe as Robin Gilmour in Milngavie tells us about one young comedian who was going down like a lead balloon and shouted in exasperation at the audience: "Am I invisible or something?" Naturally it was too good an opportunity to miss for one chap in the audience who shouted back: "Did someone say something there?"

OUR STORY about rocker Jimmy Page's birthday reminds Steve Inch in Bishopbriggs of when his pal Dean went to a Led Zeppelin concert in Aberdeen in the early 1970s.

Having two spare tickets he went into the Star and Garter Bar opposite the Aberdeen Music Hall where he spotted two potential customers having a quiet drink in the corner.

When Dean asked if they fancied buying a couple of tickets to see the show, one told him: "Sorry mate, we're the band," and at that Jimmy Page and Robert Plant finished their drinks and headed across the road to tune up.

AS THE PROTESTS continued around the world about the prison sentences in Russia for the girls from punk band Pussy Riot, Don Ferguson in London wishfully comments: "Dear Vladimir Putin, Justin Bieber and One Direction were just singing nasty songs about you."

CHRISTMAS parties continued. A reader in a late-night taxi queue in Glasgow heard a tipsy young woman ask her pal: "Is it getting cooler, or am I wearing fewer clothes than when I went out this evening?"

THE BIG CINEMA hit just now is *Les Miserables*. Brenda Gillies from Newport-on-Tay suppressed an urge to shout out: "The clue's in the title" when she went to see the film and "there we were in the hushed cinema, emotions wrung, breathless with the drama unfolding before us, when a loud voice shatters our concentration with the words, 'Not very cheery, is it?'"

OFFICE CHRISTMAS parties continued. A chap who was accompanied to his office do by his wife was telling friends: "I can now tell how attractive the women in my office are by the number of times my wife told me an individual looked like a tramp."

CHRISTMAS PARTY nights are in full swing at hotels around the country. Martyn James, compere and magician at The Leapark Hotel in Grangemouth, told the audience that he had changed his career to showbusiness after a serious accident. He says he suffered a broken neck – and "hasn't looked back since".

THE DAY AFTER the Christmas party one chap was telling his pal that he unfortunately told his boss he reminded him of Santa.

"That doesn't sound too bad," said his mate.

"What I actually said," replied his pal, "was that he was fat and only worked one day of the year."

WE LIKED this plaintive little posting on the T In The Park Facebook page from one of the many thousands who attended the weekend's festivities: "Gonnae help me . . . av lost my granny in the Slam tent and she's my lift home."

A READER was outside Cineworld in Glasgow where a young couple were discussing which film to go and see. The chap suggested the Pedro Almodóvar film *I'm So Excited*, which is in Spanish. But as his date argued, quite logically when you think about it: "The problem with subtitled films is that you actually have to watch them."

BRAINDEAD Theatre Company, appearing at Edinburgh Fringe with detective story *Fast Film Noir*, admit they were a bit naive when they first came to Scotland 13 years ago. Their first show was called *Cigarettes and Chocolate* and on arrival in Edinburgh they excitedly unpacked and went up the Royal Mile to publicise the show with one actor in a seven-foot foam cigarette costume.

Within minutes a member of the public put a lighter to the giant fag with the chap inside it.

NOT every couple shares the same musical tastes, of course. A woman leaving Glasgow Royal Concert Hall with her partner was heard telling him triumphantly: "Told you you'd like it."

But the chap merely replied: "I clapped because it finished, not because I liked it."

WE MENTIONED the award given to Glasgow nightclub owner Colin Barr, which reminds John McCormick of when Colin opened one of Glasgow's first gay clubs, the famous Bennets on Glassford Street. Says John: "A female friend of mine tried to enter Bennets and asked Colin how much it was to get in. When he told her she gasped and said: 'What? And I'm guaranteed not to get a lumber!' She paid up anyway and had a fab night."

MUSIC FANS have been remembering the wild nights at Glasgow's Barrowland venue, with Tony Gaughan telling us: "I got a big chunk bitten out of my hand by some mad wummin at the concert by David Bowie's Tin Machine band. My London mates thought this was hilarious as I needed a tetanus injection."

GLASGOW ODEON continued. James Johnston worked as a telegram boy out of the George Square GPO when he had to deliver a telegram to legendary American singer Connie Francis at the Odeon. James put it in a priority envelope to be delivered in person, and on being shown into her dressing room he delivered said communication and waited with hand cupped at his thigh.

But instead of a tip, all he got was a "That's all mailman."

Back at the depot when colleagues asked if he got her autograph he replied: "Get her autograph? I could'nae get two ha'pennies for a penny."

TRADITIONAL music festival Celtic Connections continues in Glasgow, with one of the performers asking his audience: "How do you get a guitar player to stop playing?" He answered himself: "Put sheet music in front of him."

AS SCOTSMEN look out their kilts for Burns suppers, many will feel sympathy with BBC presenter Mark Stephen, who compered the Celtic Connections opening concert while wearing his kilt. "It takes nine yards of material to make a kilt," he told the audience, "so how the hell can it be too tight?"

WE MENTIONED a Celtic Connections gig taking place in the unusual surroundings of Kelvingrove Art Gallery. Phil McCluskey tells us support act John Murry from Mississippi looked up at the Spitfire hung from the ceiling, down the gallery at the stuffed elephant, Sir Roger, and confided to the audience: "I've been dying to ask, why is that Spitfire chasing the elephant? Is this a British thing?"

COMEDIAN Mark Steel, who is touring Scotland later this month, always likes to include local stories in his performance. We remember when he was in Berwick-upon-Tweed and heard the apocryphal yarn that Berwick was technically still at war with Russia as its name was missed off a peace treaty hundreds of years ago.

When Mark contacted the Foreign Office to verify this, he was loftily told: "If Berwick-upon-Tweed is at war with Russia, they certainly haven't informed us."

COMEDIAN Ross Noble interrupted his show at the Glasgow Pavilion as he spotted a chap near the front looking at his phone. When Noble asked what was so important, the chap replied he was getting the latest score from the Braehead Clan ice hockey game which was currently at five goals each.

An hour later at the end of his show Ross asked the audience if they had any questions.

"What was the final score in the ice hockey?" shouted back a voice from the back.

WE DROP the curtain on our Glasgow Odeon stories with Andrew Adamson in Airdrie recalling seeing *Star Wars* as a student in the 1970s. Says Andrew: "Sitting as the opening scenes rolled and the huge spaceship passed overhead, the whole auditorium rumbled and I could feel my seat vibrate. I was very impressed with this new 'sensurround' effect.

"It was years later that I realised it was the rumble of a train entering Queen Street Station low level."

9
Going Down The Pub

Fortunately Scots don't just go to the pub for a drink. They tell some good tales as well.

PARENTING skills Glasgow-style. A chap meeting his pals in the pub said he had to feed his year-old son spaghetti bolognaise before he came out. "So to save time," he told them, "I did what my son would have done – I threw half of it on the carpet."

"I TOOK a bookmaker's daughter out the other night," said the chap in the Glasgow pub. "The bookie thought he was a bit of a comedian – told me she had to be home at ten to one."

THE CHAP in the Glasgow pub was being bought drinks by mates after his wife had given birth. Recounting the event, he told them: "When the wife was in labour the nurse came in and said: 'How about epidural anaesthesia?' So I told her, Naw you're alright hen, we've already picked a name."

LOVERS of nostalgia should note that Kestrel Lager, the green-canned liquid which was always the last to be drunk at 1970s parties, is to be brewed again in Glasgow – hopefully to a new recipe.

When English rapper Tinie Tempah released a track with the lines: "My uncle used to drink a can of Kestrel, when life got stressful" a fan remarked: "If he's the kind of man who drinks Kestrel, the only stressful thing in his life is making sure the cardboard box he lives in doesn't blow away."

THE DISCUSSION in a Glasgow pub the other night was about the rising cost of living. Eventually one punter declared: "When I was young I was scared of the dark. Now when I see my electricity bill I'm scared of the lights."

AUTHOR Alasdair Smith's debut crime novel *The Unfaithful Seven* has episodes from Glasgow pubs – including one he witnessed himself in one of the city's more challenging east end venues.

A local patron walked in with a carrier bag, handed it to the barman, and asked him to place it on top of the fridge for safekeeping.

Says Alasdair: "It is of enormous credit to the barman that when he looked inside and spotted the snake coiled up he accepted that the warmth and vibration from the fridge would keep the snake calm while the patron finished his drink."

WE MENTIONED the reincarnation of Kestrel lager which will now, curiously enough, be brewed at the Tennent's brewery in Glasgow. As Jim McDonald in Carluke recalls: "When Kestrel was originally sold by Scottish & Newcastle in the early 1980s it was launched as a competitor to Tennent's lager.

"I was working at Tennent's at the time. There was a rumour that so much unsold Kestrel was being returned to S&N it was nicknamed Homing Pigeon."

READER Dominic Gribben was in an Irvine alehouse where two of the locals were discussing their bets that day with one informing the other that he had put his cash on a horse called Lewy the Pooey. Looking up at the TV screen Dominic noticed that the nag was in fact named Louis the Pious, but not wanting to get into a long conversation with the locals about ninth century French monarchists, he decided to let it go.

"I WAS reading this great crime novel I took out the library," said the chap in the Glasgow pub at the weekend. "But halfway through I realised there were some pages missing."

After a pause he added: "I lost the plot."

BRUCE HENDERSON in Maybole was visiting a Glasgow pub when a chap there announced: "Ah'm goin to ma daugh'ers fur ma dinner, ah always go there on a Monday."

This communication was absorbed by his pals until one of them announced: "But don't you know this is Tuesday?!"

"Ach, she disnae mind if ah'm a wee bit late," the chap replied.

IT IS ALSO the time of amateur drinkers in the pubs, getting in the way of regular topers. A group of girls was dithering over their drinks selection in a Glasgow bar when the chap behind them told his pal: "How can they not know what they want to drink? I've known since I got to work this morning what I wanted to drink eight hours later."

A TOPER in a Glasgow pub at the weekend told his pals: "I thought I would make an omelette by using the food mixer, but I forgot to put the lid on properly. Boy did I end up with egg on my face."

THE SCENE: a quiz night at Arthurlie Bowling Club. One of the questions: The song 'Sit Down, You're Rocking The Boat' comes from which musical? The hopeful answer: *Titanic*

A CHAP in a Glasgow pub was being asked by his pals how his date with a dentist had gone. "She said she had a great time," he told them, "and that she would like to see me again in about six months."

EVERYONE is now sensitive about the content of food. David Watson was in a pub near Glasgow's Kelvingrove Art Gallery which was advertising "Partick Pies" and he asked the barman what they were. Trying to reassure him, the barman replied: "There's naebdy frae Partick in thae pies, pal."

ELECTRONIC cigarettes were being discussed in a Glasgow pub the other night, with one chap claiming he could smoke an ordinary cigarette but claim it was an electronic one, and thus beat the pub smoking ban. "One problem with that," his pal told him. "You roll your own."

THE GLASGOW Comedy Festival began with more than 100,000 tickets available for more than 400 shows. Glasgow lawyer turned comedian Susan Calman, appearing at The Stand, says she likes the honesty of Glaswegians. After appearing on TV show *Have I Got News for You*, she went into her South Side local – "no food, no music, no fun, but the barmaid goes to the bookie's for you" – where she was beckoned over by two wizened old regulars who told her they'd seen her on the telly, and added: "You weren't as awful as we thought you'd be."

A GROUP of Glasgow chaps in the pub at the weekend were recounting tales of lost weekends when they went out for a drink and ended up wakening the next day in a strange town or even a strange country.

   Their tales were topped by one man who declared: "I went to my 21st, got bladdered, and when I woke up I had three kids and was 50 years old."

10
Travel

Travel broadens the mind, and increases the funny stories.

A RAIN-SOAKED Clarkston reader getting the bus into work yesterday heard the girl in front of him tell her pal: "I've discovered lots of features on my laptop that I never knew existed." She then added: "Only because Tipsy my cat walked across the keyboard."

A YOUNG reader taking the bus from Edinburgh to St Andrews watched as a fellow passenger approached the driver when it stopped at Glenrothes bus station and asked if they had reached St Andrews.

The driver confirmed it was in fact Glenrothes, then added in explanation: "If St Andrews looked like this, no-one would visit it."

NEWS that Loganair is to halt flights from Dundee to Belfast reminds Brenda Gillies of when she was on the inaugural flight from Dundee and, to celebrate the event the stewardess asked: "Would youse like a glass of Buckfast?" Says Brenda: "When I suggested she perhaps meant bucks fizz, given the orange juice/cava combo on offer, the reply came, 'Oh s***, so I do.'" Ah, the glamour of domestic flight.

TALKING of stewardesses, Felix McCoy, retired head concierge at the unforgettable Albany Hotel in Glasgow, tells us they once had an American flight attendant who asked if there was a spiritualist church nearby. Felix sent a young concierge to make inquiries. He returned with directions to the spiritualist centre in Somerset Place, then added with a straight face: "Remember, ring the bell when you go there. Don't knock on the door. That just confuses them."

A READER who was moving house couldn't get over the number of boxes of books he had to pack for the removal men – particularly as he was being charged per box.

His mood wasn't helped by the foreman of the removal men who looked at the boxes and remarked: "Aye, I bet you wish the Kindle was invented a good few years earlier."

SO WHY should women know much about car mechanics? We only ask as a worker at Glasgow's most famous chain of car show-rooms tells us a woman customer was having her car repaired only to be told by the wee Glasgow mechanic: "Yer heid gasket's blew." She then asked him: "What colour should it be?"

OUR TALE of the Glasgow mechanic telling the woman "Your gasket's blew" leading to her asking him what colour it should be, provokes a Bearsden reader: "My wife said the chap in the garage had terrible amnesia. When I asked why, she said she had rung up about getting a replacement battery for her Corsa and he asked her what year it was."

BAD WEATHER has been disrupting some ferry services around Scotland. But not everyone has felt the cancellations were necessary. David Kelso was at a newsagents in Brodick, Arran, at the weekend where a sign stuck to the door stated in bright red ink: "No papers." Added in explanation below was: "You may think it's not windy, I may think it's not windy, but the CalMac psychic decided yesterday at lunchtime there was a chance a seagull might fart causing a sudden gust of wind."

THE SMEDDUM TEST, an anthology of award-winning contemporary Scottish poetry, includes Sheila Templeton's 'Last Train to Ayr' which she wrote after being unable to get on a train to Ayr from Glasgow as it was packed with Scottish football fans after a game at Hampden.

Says Sheila: "It was just impossible to squeeze another body in. Nothing unusual in that, of course, but as I stood there on the platform, extremely frustrated, I had to laugh, watching the train ticket man literally running along, physically pushing in big bellies so that the electronic doors would close. I'd never seen anyone do that before."

NORMALLY people speaking loudly on their mobile phones on trains can be very annoying to fellow travellers. But Tom Rafferty, who caught the very early train to London from Glasgow the other day, could only feel sympathy for the chap near him, as the train passed Preston around nine o'clock, who bellowed down his phone: "Cancelled? How do you mean, cancelled? I'm on the 0630 for this!"

WE HEAR of a rail passenger at Glasgow's Central Station waiting for the train to Wemyss Bay who needed the loo. Just then a train from Ayr pulled in, so he jumped on board to use the on-train facilities.

Locked inside the loo, however, the lights suddenly went out as the train was being taken out of service and the driver had locked it up. Trapped in Stygian darkness he managed to pull the toilet doors open before his cries for help were heard by a passing station cleaner who used an emergency key to let him out.

And he still made the Wemyss Bay train with seconds to spare.

OUR STORY of buying a return ticket reminds David Witton in Helensburgh of taking the Western Ferries boat from Gourock to Dunoon, and wanting to know the price difference in fares before deciding whether to take the long, scenic route back by road, or simply catch the ferry.

Says David: "When the purser appeared at the car to collect the fares I asked him, 'Can you tell me the difference between a single and a return?' His quick retort was, 'Sir, with a return you get to come back again.'"

WE LIKED the tweet from Milton Jones, who is appearing at the Assembly Hall at the Edinburgh Fringe, who tweeted: "Heh heh. tweeting on board airplane in sky. They said it would mess up th."

THERE is an endless debate on whether reliance on new technology has left youngsters unable to cope. John Duffy tells us: "My friend was on a train from Manchester, sharing the carriage with a large number of young people who had been at a music festival. One lad asked what time the train would get to York. Nobody knew exactly, but my friend gave him the timetable she had picked up in Manchester. He stared at it for a second or two, then handed it back to her, saying, 'You'll need to show me how this works.'"

POLITICAL activist and comedian Mark Thomas was in Glasgow this week for the Great May Day Cabaret he was performing in at Glasgow's Oran Mor. We can all feel his pain as he tweeted from his train heading south the next day: "Teens playing Beyonce through mini speakers on train. Tempted to dance in the aisle next to them shouting, 'I love this one!'"

MORE on car keys: a reader was at a plant nursery – I know, how optimistic in this weather – when a customer announced she had locked her keys in the car.

A nursery worker said he would fetch something that would help, and returned with a large hammer in his hand.

The customer fearfully urged him not to use it, but the worker replied: "No, not that!" and showed her the mobile phone he was carrying in his other hand.

CAR KEYS continued. Mungo Henning's sister locked her keys in her car and pleaded to her hubby for help. Says Mungo: "He disappeared into the house and returned with a three-foot length of fencing wire. Then he went up to the door of the highly secure Saab and while obscuring what he was up to, opened the door in about 10 seconds.

"My sister, delighted at the problem being solved was nevertheless aghast at the dubious skills required to achieve it. She quizzed her husband along the lines of 'where on earth did you learn to do that?' "At that point he produced the spare keys from his trouser pocket, fetched from the house along with the smokescreen of the fencing wire."

GLASGOW'S taxi drivers showed their caring side with the annual children's outing to Troon. One driver was resplendent in a full Mickey Mouse costume, complete with mouse head.

But as one of his fellow drivers told him: "That's the best you've looked in a long time. I'd keep that on if I was you."

TALKING of airports, a reader says he was travelling back from Dublin when there was a bit of a stushie in the security queue in front of him.

Eventually he heard the security chap tell a confused woman: "No, you don't put your baby on the tray. You can take him straight through with you."

NOT EVERYONE in Glasgow is a cycling fan, despite the crowds who turned out for Mark Cavendish winning the British National Road Race in Glasgow. As reader Robin Gilmour remarks: "Mr Cavendish and his fellow cyclists must have been extremely frustrated by all those cheering Glaswegians preventing them from cycling on the pavements."

WE MENTIONED going on cruises, and Graeme Allan in Rothesay recalls hearing a woman discussing cruising with a friend on the Greenock train to Glasgow. The friend was very keen on them, but the woman was not convinced as she eventually conceded: "Aye, they're lovely big boats, but I wouldnae go overboard."

"I really wanted to tell her that wasn't the idea," says Graeme.

MENTION of the Glasgow to Edinburgh Citylink bus reminds James Beyer in Edinburgh of being on the service and overhearing two excitable French girls near the front having a conversation in their native tongue, with one exclaiming, "Oui! Oui!" after her pal's chat.

The bus driver also heard her and helpfully pointed out to them where the toilet was located near the back of the bus.

TRAIN tickets continued. David Campbell from Helensburgh had arrived in Edinburgh's Waverley Station for the rugby at Murrayfield and noticed the taxi queue was a mile long. As his pal had been ill and couldn't manage the long walk to the stadium, they decided to catch a train to Haymarket instead – a journey so short it is rarely undertaken.

Says David: "The ticket clerk seemed unimpressed with our travel plans, as indicated by an audible tut and a rolling of the eyes. As he handed us two single tickets to Haymarket, he enquired, 'Dae yiz want tae book a sleeper?'"

DAFT gag from the weekend? "My mate rang me and asked: 'What are you doing at the moment?' I said: 'Probably failing my driving test.'"

BUS conversations continued. A Stirling reader heard a teenager tell her pals with some sadness: "My life is a constant cycle of waiting for the weekend, and then doing nothing when it comes."

DONALD GRANT in Paisley ventured out in a new trapper-style fur hat, feeling a bit self-conscious as it wasn't normal west-of-Scotland headgear.

Says Donald: "I was standing at the bus stop in the driving sleet waiting to go to Paisley. When a bus came, the driver opened the door and called, 'In ye come son. Ah've got a hat like that and ah look ridiculous as well.'

"Whether I wear it again is still debatable."

DAVID BROWNLEE recounts a friend who had to take his new expensive car back to the dealer as its alarm was going off for no reason. Says David: "Three trips to the dealer and lots of scratching of heads did not solve the problem for, as usual, the problem did not arise in the garage.

"That night his wife asked if he had fitted the kitchen smoke alarm she had thoughtfully placed in his toolbox in the boot of his car so he would not forget to do so."

CALUM McNICOL was flying from Glasgow to London City airport when it was announced that both the pilot and first officer were female. The flight of course went without incident until they arrived when the purser eventually announced to frustrated passengers: "We're very sorry, ladies and gentlemen, for the delay in disembarking. The ground crew are in the process of repositioning the passenger stairs."

The chap behind Calum couldn't stop himself from declaring: "I telt ye. She might have driven down here okay, but I knew she wouldn't be able to park."

BUS drivers continued. Donald Grant in Paisley tells us: "I was travelling from the Royal Alexandra Hospital to Paisley Cross when the driver stopped for a drunk at a bus stop. When he opened the door the guy shouted in, 'Hey driver do you know where this bus is gauin'?' 'Naw,' was the harassed reply and he drove off much to the great amusement of his passengers."

OFFICE parties are in full swing, which is why a south-side reader found himself in a large taxi queue outside Central Station at one in the morning at the weekend. "The wait was entertained," he tells us, "by an inebriated young woman in an impossibly short glittery dress screeching at her pal: 'Ah found yer nose. It wiz in ma business again.'"

A GLASGOW reader swears that he overheard a young chap on the bus the other day tell his pal: "My neighbours listen to some excellent music.

"Whether they want to or not."

STRANGE are the things that happen at bus stops. A south-side reader was at Buchanan Bus Station in Glasgow where a young father was playing with his toddler son before he stopped to read the bus timetable. He then suddenly looked around frantically and said to the woman with him: "Where's the boy gone?" The woman shook her head and replied: "He's still sitting on your shoulders."

Yes, he had indeed forgotten he had swung the little one across his back.

OUR TESCO stories remind Mungo Henning: "While dropping my car off at a back-street garage for some work, I bemoaned the fact that I had lost a hub cap and wondered where I could buy a single one, and not a set of four. The mechanic suggested Tesco.

"My puzzled look was met by his following words, 'The car park, not the shop.'"

WE ASKED for your removal stories, and Allan Mackintosh recounts: "When we moved from Glasgow to Troon, my wife approached one of the removal lads at the new house to ask if they could remove a very large spider from one of the bedrooms. 'Sorry hen, we don't do livestock' was his dead-pan reply."

REMOVALS continued. Ian Forrest in Laurencekirk reminds us of the removal van driver who stopped in Brechin some years ago and asked a local woman where a certain street was. She didn't know, but as she had lived there all her life, she took his delivery sheet, read it, and told him: "You do know you're supposed to be in Brecon in Wales?"

A STIRLINGSHIRE reader tells us the foreman in charge of his removal was fed up with the young lad in the crew constantly asking what he should do next. Eventually the foreman told him: "You go in the wardrobe to hold the coat-hangers steady while we carry it downstairs."

Our reader says the youngster was opening the wardrobe door before he realised the foreman was joking.

GREAT to see the paddle steamer *Waverley* still puffing away on the Clyde. A reader tells us that as part of its fundraising efforts, the *Waverley* folk are selling off one of its anchors with a minimum bid of £1,800. When a passenger asked if that was not a wee bit expensive for an anchor, a crew member told him that "it was really just a drop in the ocean."

BOYS can be so cruel to each other. This was confirmed by a reader on a bus into Glasgow who heard a teenage chap ask his pal: "Can I borrow your phone to give my girlfriend a bell." "Sure," replied his mate, handing his mobile over. "Just press redial."

A RENFREWSHIRE reader at the Duty Free shop at Glasgow Airport read the sign at the door which proudly proclaimed: "More than you would imagine." He tells us that after looking at their prices, he couldn't agree more.

OUR GEORGE SQUARE tales remind entertainer Andy Cameron of his early days as a bus conductor on the night service from George Square to Castlemilk. Says Andy: "Upstairs a wee drunk guy informs me that he had 'nae money' so, being me, I asked if he could sing. 'Nae bother' says he and gets right into his song 'Hullo Hullo'. Haud oan' says me, it's a mixed company – ye canny sing a Rangers song. He just ignored me and carried on with the next line, 'Who's yer lady friend.'"

11
Work

Some folk swear they go to work more for the laughs than the wages.

OUR TALE of the woman who blamed her laughter lines on all the clowns she had dated, reminds David Robertson out in Marrakech: "I used to tease one of the nurses I worked with with the line: look at all your wee wrinkles. She said: 'They're not wrinkles they're laughter lines', to which I replied: Nothing's that funny."

CLYDE shipyard worker Bob Starrett has published a collection of stories and cartoons about the yards in his book *The Way I See It*. One involves Wee Bunty and her team, who had polished off a half-bottle in the yard. Wishing to continue the impromptu session, Bunty volunteered to get more drink, and asked a painter to fill up the empty bottle with turps. No, they weren't going to drink it. Instead Bunty took it to the off-licence where she had bought the original half-bottle and asked the shop owner to smell it.

He did so, conceded there was something wrong with it, and handed over a new half-bottle.

A CHAP was in his work canteen in Livingston when the woman serving was complaining to her fellow worker that the flesh on her upper arm had lost its muscle tone.

Despite the queue of folk waiting she jiggled her arm and announced: "I'm thinking of getting a Saltire tattooed on it – then it would look like it was flapping in the wind."

NICKNAMES – Martin Shields in Australia recalls: "I had a manager who was nicknamed The Mirror because any time you asked him about a decision or a problem, he said, 'I'll look into it.'"

NICKNAMES continued. Andy Jamieson in Bearsden tells us about the newsagent in Kirkcudbright who was fed up with the mayhem and occasional thieving caused by schoolkids at lunchtime. Says Andy: "After the rush he would retire to his local pub where he would regale anyone who would listen about how much he hated these kids, the stress they caused him and what he would do to them if he caught them stealing. He went on to such an extent that the locals nicknamed him Herod."

OUR STORIES of Burns suppers and haggis remind Kirsty Buchanan of applying for a job in England. "The application said: 'If you were an animal what animal would you be and why?' I wrote: 'A haggis, so I could run free in the beautiful highland hillsides.' I was invited for an interview. The interviewer said: 'I only invited you to see if you really thought a haggis was an animal.' To which I pointed out I had only written it to see if he did. I got the job."

THE DEBATE continues on whether home working or office working is the best. Comedian Susan Calman does her writing at home. And, as she observed at the Glasgow Comedy Festival: "Told my cat to beat it, and stop putting his tail in my cup of tea.

"I miss working in an office. No-one ever put their a*** in my tea there."

THE CHAP in the Glasgow pub the other night told his pals: "I was down the Jobcentre where the woman behind the counter berated me, saying: 'You're always late, you ignore the queue of people, and you are rude to everyone.' She then asked if I'd ever thought of becoming a bus driver."

DIFFICULT time, applying for jobs these days. A reader heard a young chap in Glasgow yesterday tell his pal: "They asked me if I did any sports and I told them surfing. Missed out 'the internet' of course."

TALKING of banking and the difficulties of raising finance, Andy Leven remembers when his father ran a butcher's shop in Dennistoun in the sixties and had a notice on the wall which stated "CREFDIT". It allowed him, of course, when a puzzled customer said there was no F in Credit, to reply: "Exactly."

IT'S TRICKY meeting someone from your past. Jim Morrison tells us about a pal who was in the Braehead shopping centre when he saw a familiar face, but couldn't quite place the chap.

He asked him if he had worked in Babcock's which he confirmed. So Jim's pal breenged on: "Do you remember that foreman who was always spying on us, a specky sod?"

"Yes," said the chap. "That was me – wear contacts now."

A GLASGOW reader thinks the student working in the office for the summer will go far. When the student's boss asked him to do something, the young chap replied: "So when do you want this by? Yesterday or an hour ago?"

DAFT GAG of the week? A reader tells us: "I'm looking to start up my own business, recycling discarded chewing gum. "Just need help getting it off the ground."

THE HEAD of a company's human resources department swears to us a chap was asked at a job interview the standard question: "What do you think is your greatest weakness?" "Honesty," he replied. "I don't think honesty is a weakness," he was told. "I don't care what you think," he responded.

A LONDON reader tells us about an announcement made over his office's public address system that a pair of glasses had been found and handed in to reception.

The announcer added: "If they are yours, please come and pick them up at reception," then added after a pause: "If you can find your way there."

A GLASGOW office worker tells us a young Polish girl has joined the team, and is putting everyone to shame by always being the first to arrive every morning. She's been given the nickname Krakow Dawn.

OUR READER unsure of wearing a fur hat reminds John Daly of a manager at British Steel who announced that he had been given one of these "Russian-style furry hats for Christmas."

Says John: "New Year came and went, and someone asked him why we hadn't seen him with it on. He said, 'I feel a wee bit self-conscious about wearing it. So, I'm wearing it in the hoose until I get used to it.'"

A NEW exhibition on the history of Scotch whisky which has just opened at Glasgow's Mitchell Library reminds David Donaldson of the scam a while back of farmers fond of a dram who would buy generous quantities of the smooth, blended malt whisky Sheep Dip and put it through the farm's books as a tax- and VAT-deductible expense.

THE CLYDE shipyard stories of Bob Starrett inevitably remind Andy Cameron of Jimmy "The Pig" McCrindle who was a renowned shipyard joker in the sixties.

Says Andy: "He used to come to the Rolls-Royce Club when I was compere and do an Al Jolson turn with a few stories about the yards.

"A favourite of mine was 'Ah wis workin' away the other day when the gaffer comes up an' says, 'Is that whisky ah can smell on your breath McCrindle?' It better be, says I or that licensed grocer is gettin' a doin.'"

A GLASGOW businessman, through in Edinburgh for a dinner organised by accountancy giants Ernst and Young for the country's captains of industry, noticed two company chairmen tapping excitedly on their smartphones at the end of the evening. Were they checking share prices or seeking out the latest news headlines? No, they intimated that as they were over 60, they used their free bus passes, and were searching the Lothian bus app on their phones to see when the bus they wanted would go past the Caledonian Hotel.

PRONOUNCING names continued. Architect Robert Menzies tells us: "When telephoning a London firm for a product catalogue, a sales assistant with a pronounced 'Souf London' accent answered. Given the problems I have with my surname in England, I carefully spelt out M-E-N-Z-I-E-S over the phone, adding 'and it's R for Robert.' I duly received a parcel the next day addressed to Mr Arfur Robert Menzies."

A CHAP in a Glasgow pub at the weekend was telling his mates about a job interview which he thought didn't go well. "They asked me to sum myself up in three words. And for some reason I replied, 'Really rubbish at maths.'"

THE BOSS in a Glasgow office asked a young member of staff to find him a bulldog clip. The youngster emailed him a YouTube video of one wearing a Union Flag bowler hat.

BOB BLACK, now in Elgin, tells us: "Working at the Gray Dunn factory in Scotland Street during summer vacation from university in the seventies, I was intrigued when assigned to the 'wafer room'.

"It's name soon became clear at break-time when the gaffer sidled up and said, 'wafer a smoke, big man.'"

YOU CAN'T be too careful, it seems. NHS Grampian has launched a website giving advice on sexual health. Due to the graphic nature of some of the advice it has now told its own staff they should not attempt to access the site using an NHS Grampian computer.

A WISHAW reader confesses he didn't know why his mobile phone was broken after his office night out. It only became clear when he went back to work and a colleague asked him if he recalled putting his mobile onto airplane mode and then trying to fly it across the room.

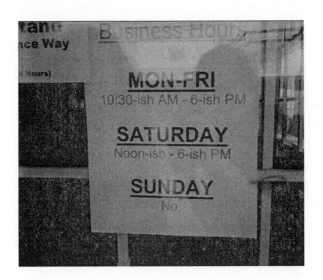

WE HEAR about the new apprentice at a south-side of Glasgow garage who had been warned by his father to watch out for the mechanics playing practical jokes on him, such as sending him for a tin of tartan paint. His first week was going well until the foreman shouted over to him to pass him a monkey wrench. The lad thought about this before replying: "A monkey wrench? Do you think I'm stupid? There's no such thing."

DAFT GAG of the weekend? The chap in the Glasgow pub who declared: "My son's taking a course in engraving. I asked him after the first day if he had learned much, but he said they had hardly scratched the surface."

12
Children and Grandparents

As a grandfather once said, the great thing about grandchildren is you hand them back at the end of the day.

A BEARSDEN reader tempted out by the sun to do the first gardening of the year tells us that last summer his granddaughter raced in to tell him that there were a large number of snails on the garden path. Thinking of a well-known remedy, our reader announced: "I'll get some salt."

"You're not going to eat them?" screeched a horrified granddaughter.

STRANGE how things that were once the norm now seem so alien. A Bearsden mum tells us her son was visiting his granny where he was puzzled by a small, lumpy piece of material, and asked what it was. "A pin cushion," replied gran. "Why do you want to make your pins comfortable?" he asked.

A READER swears he was in a crowded Byres Road, Glasgow, at the West End Festival yesterday when he heard a young lad ask the woman holding his hand: "Mummy, why is your bottom so big?" The woman kept her composure and merely replied: "That's not a polite thing to ask."

The lad thought about this before trying again: "Why is your bottom so big, please?"

A MILNGAVIE teenager was asked by her parents what she would like for her seventeenth birthday, and she replied a tad hopefully: "Something I can drive." "A golf ball doesn't cost much," replied her dad.

A GLASGOW teacher tells us he is already looking forward to the Christmas break after telling one of his pupils this week that she was late for class. "A queen is never late," she serenely replied. "Everyone else is simply early."

WE NOTICE that Glasgow author Allan Morrison has brought out a book on the sayings of Glasgow grannies, *Haud ma Chips, Ah've Drapped the Wean*, which includes the tart advice given to children who don't get their own way: "Ah could hang oot ma washing oan that petted lip."

AN EXASPERATED mother in Hyndland saw her teenage daughter hanging about the house and asked what her plans were for the day. "Nothing," the girl replied. "That's what you did yesterday," said her mum. "Not finished it yet," came the reply.

HALLOWEEN, and Lynda Nicholson recalls: "It was pouring one Halloween when I lived in Clarkston, so to protect my new carpets from all the dirty feet, I put a rug down and told all the guisers they had to stand on it to do their jokes and songs. Before I knew it I had a queue down the path. I had no idea why my house was so popular until the next day when I heard it was the best to go to 'because it had a stage.'"

KINSHIP CARE is helping family members, often grandparents, who bring up children. One couple told Children 1st: "When our granddaughter first came to stay with us she told social workers we had given her bones for her tea. It was actually spare ribs!"

OUR STORIES of grandparents encouraged a reader to retell the classic, that is, old, story of the granddaughter out in the country with her gran who suddenly said: "Look at all these coos!" Gran, keen to improve her vocabulary, told the little one: "Not coos – cows."

The young girl thought about this before replying: "Well they look like coos to me."

A READER on the train to Glasgow from Clydebank heard a teenager tell her pal about her sister having a baby. She added: "She then gave me the baby to hold. And when you think how often I've dropped my phone, that was pretty brave of her."

A BEARSDEN reader tells us his neighbour, who is a doctor, felt a warm glow when he was driving his young daughter to school and she picked up his stethoscope and put it in her ears. Just as he was thinking it was a sign she also wanted to enter the medical profession, she spoke into it: "Welcome to McDonalds. May I take your order?"

A BISHOPBRIGGS reader tells us his teenage daughter was excited about her comfortable and warm onesie outfit that she had bought, and she wondered aloud if they would ever catch on with men. "We wore them when we were young," her grandfather piped up from behind his newspaper. "Only we called them overalls."

"WHERE do you begin?" wonders a reader as he hears an upset teenager in a Glasgow clothing store tell her mum: "It's not fair, I bet gran never took your iPhone away from you when you went to bed."

A READER tells us his daughter's magazine had been asking celebrities various inane questions including: "If you could have any superpower, what would it be?" He was taken with the chap who replied: "China."

A MARYHILL reader was in the supermarket when she heard a young lad shout at his big brother: "It's my birthday. You said you'd be nice to me today!" But the bigger lad replied in brotherly fashion: "No, I said I wouldn't hurt you today."

A READER tells us he heard a young girl walking down Byres Road in Glasgow ask her pals: "Do you think I'm vain?" She then added before they could reply: "It's just that I read in a magazine article that really good-looking people often are."

GRANDCHILDREN continued. Douglas McLeod in New-lands, Glasgow recalls a friend's five-year-old daughter visiting her grandmother who had no sweets in the house and instead gave the child an oatcake covered with jam as a treat.

A few minutes later the little girl appeared back in the kitchen with the uneaten oatcake on the plate, now minus the jam, and announced: "Thanks for the jam Granny – and here's your wee board back."

OUR MENTION of the Glasgow Science Centre reminded Kate Woods: "I once worked in research at a museum. Many complex questions landed on my desk, requiring extensive research to give an adequate answer. But the most memorable question I got was from a small child who asked, 'Is the dead mouse part of the exhibit?'"

A BISHOPBRIGGS reader passes on a verbal tussle between a harassed mother and her recalcitrant child at the local shops with the youngster defiantly stating: "You call it talking back. I just call it explaining."

AN ANNIESLAND reader smiled to herself as she heard a teen-age girl on her train tell the school pals with her: "I'm always exaggerating. I must exaggerate about 1,000 times a day."

KIDS can be difficult when you are shopping. A reader at the supermarket heard a fed-up wee boy moan at his mum that he wanted to go home.

Trying to placate him, the mum told him: "We'll just get bread and then we'll go home." But he yelled: "I want to go home now. I don't want bread. I only want toast."

WE ASKED about the joys of being a grandparent, and a grandmother in Clarkston tells us she was putting on her make-up under the watchful eye of her little granddaughter.

When she automatically dabbed off any excess lipstick with a piece of toilet paper, the little girl asked: "Nan, why do you kiss the toilet paper goodbye?"

A READER was pondering on the more unusual names parents are giving their children these days.

"Do you think," he tells us, "in twenty years' time a hard-working woman gets home, collapses in a chair and tells her husband, 'There's a bottle of wine with my name on it.' And he replies, 'Of course there is Chardonnay.'"

MORE grandchildren stories as Jim McDougall tells us: "My sister-in-law in Greenock was bathing her three-year-old granddaughter who asked: 'What was I like when I was born, Granny?' Granny replied that she was very small and only four pounds, whereupon the tot exclaimed, 'What, did Mummy have to buy me?'"

WHEN did Mothering Sunday become Mother's Day? Anyway, we fervently hope the two children overheard in the supermarket at Silverburn near Glasgow on Saturday didn't disappoint their mum. A reader shopping there heard the little boy and girl discussing what to buy their mother when the girl said: "We could get her some bath stuff."

The boy looked puzzled as he replied: "What? Bleach?"

"SILENCE is golden," a woman having coffee with friends in the West End was heard to observe. "Unless you have kids – then it's just suspicious."

SCENES from a Glasgow park – Jim Evans had taken his four-year-old granddaughter to the park, where she climbed to the top of a big chute, but then decided she didn't want to slide down. Still not moving after much cajoling, she stood at the top while grandad moved to the ladder to climb up to help her and was abruptly told by the wee boy at the front of the queue: "It's no' yer turn."

"I'm going next," pleaded Jim, only to be met with a "Naw y'urny." Which is why a red-faced grandfather slunk to the back of the queue.

ON the subject of squirrels – we hear of a minister who was taking the Sunday School when he asked the children: "What am I? I'm small, I'm furry, I've got a big tail and I like to eat nuts."

A girl put up her hand, squirmed and – obviously wrestling with a heavy burden – answered: "I know it should be Jesus. But is it a squirrel?"

WE MENTIONED charity Children 1st collecting grandparents' stories to highlight how involved they often are in childcare. One supporter told them: "My grandma loved to tell jokes but could never get the punchline right. My favourite was the classic, 'Why did the beetroot blush?' and the little response she got when she added, 'Because it saw the mayonnaise'. The punchline should have been of course, 'Because it saw the salad dressing.'"

DAFT gag of the day? A young lad in Govan told his mum if she paid him a quid, he'd be good for the rest of the day. "I shouldn't have to pay you to be good," his mother replied. "You should be good for nothin' – just like yer faither."

A PRIMARY school teacher tells us she has often wondered if any of her primary one charges go home after their first day and tell their parents: "I'm just wasting my time there. I can't read, I can't write, and they won't let me talk."

A READER tells us his little granddaughter came home from primary school before the summer break and revealed she had kissed a boy in her class.

When our reader asked why, she replied that the boy had been bugging her, and she knew if she kissed him he would run off and leave her alone.

Might not work that way when she's a bit older, grandad cautioned.

MORE grandparents' stories. Mark Johnston tells us: "When I was a student, I phoned my gran on her birthday. On a whim, I put on a silly voice and said, 'Hello Mrsh Johnshton your grandshun has shent you a shinging telegram' and proceeded to sing 'Happy Birthday' in the same voice.

"I'd assumed she knew it was me but later that day I got a call from her thanking me so much for her singing telegram. 'Mind you', she said, 'you should ask for your money back – he couldn't sing for toffee.'"

LYN McLEAN in Stirling tells us: "In the sixties, my cousin Jimmy was sitting with Granny while she was writing a letter to relatives in Canada. Granny told Jimmy: 'I'm tellin' them aboot ye playin' the banjo in thon band with yir friends.' Jimmy, his street cred affronted replied: 'It's not a banjo, Granny!' 'Ah ken it's no', son, but Ah canny spell ukulele', she said."

A READER in Silverburn Shopping Centre didn't know whether to be impressed or appalled by the youngster, only about six, who was told by his exasperated mother: "Stop that! And I'm not going to tell you again!" The little one came back with: "Good. I was getting bored hearing you say that."

13
Where Is The Third World Country

Politicians – you really do have to laugh at them.

THE LATEST TV fun is voting to have bug-frightened Tory MP Nadine Dorries, currently in the Australian rainforest as part of *I'm A Celebrity Get Me Out of Here,* carry out the gruesome tasks at which she struggles.

As Orkney and Shetland Liberal Democrat MP Alistair Carmichael put it: "You have to think that if voting for Tories was this much fun normally, Scotland would have more than one Tory MP."

THE SCOTTISH political news is that First Minister Alex Salmond has put Nicola Sturgeon in charge of the independence campaign and promoted no-nonsense Alex Neil in her place. As former Labour spin doctor Bill Heaney put it: "Salmond's now between a frock and a hard case."

THE TRAGI-COMEDY play *I, Tommy* about disgraced Pollok politician Tommy Sheridan was on at the Glasgow King's. Des

McLean says he has the perfect title if they ever make the play into a film. He would want it to be called The *Pollokshawshank Redemption*.

BRUCE SKIVINGTON was shocked by the news story that Tory MP Sir Tony Baldry had crashed his Mercedes into a portable toilet and then hit a Poundland shop in Banbury, Oxfordshire. "Totally unbelievable," says Bruce. "A Poundland in Oxfordshire?"

FORMER Scottish Labour leader Jack McConnell, passing the time as snow delayed his flight, asked his Twitter followers for film ideas suited to his native Ayrshire. The puns flooded in. We particularly liked *Some Auchinleck It Hot*, the *Onthank Redemption*, *Natural Sorn Killers*, to *Kill a Mauchline Bird*, and *The Witches of Prestwick*.

THE GOVERNMENT'S welfare changes are still causing furious debate. A reader tells us: "A smug guy at a west-end party was trying to chat up a young woman. When she asked him what he did for a living he asked her to guess and gave her a clue that he sat around all day doing nothing at the taxpayers' expense. She thought for a moment, then asked: "Unemployed, politician or royalty?"

AMERICAN comedian Scott Capurro gave on outsider's view on Scotland while appearing at The Stand in the Glasgow Comedy Festival. "Scotland has all this oil," he pointed out. "And all you want to do with it is deep fry everything."

ALEX SALMOND gives the date for the independence referendum. Perusing the details on the BBC website, a reader notes that someone left the comment at the end of the story: "Let's all hope that sense prevails, and a Third World country isn't created on our doorstep."

Says our reader: "It would have helped if the person leaving the comment had stated whether they were in England or Scotland."

AS WE deliberate what lasting effect the Chris Huhne and Vicky Pryce court case will have on British politics and our understanding of crime and punishment, a reader brings us back down to earth by telling us: "I hear HM Prison Holloway women's football team has a new proven penalty taker."

A TEACHER tells us he was holding mock parliamentary elections in his modern studies class when the class clown insisted on standing for the Pyjama Party arguing: "Who wouldn't want to vote for a pyjama party?"

FORMER Glasgow MP George Galloway was in the news for storming out of an Oxford University debate as he refused to share the platform with an Israeli student. It reminds us of the chap who declared: "Someone said I suffer from xenophobia, whatever that is. I bet you I caught it off some foreigner."

HOWARD TINDALL reads the book about Poland during the Second World War, *The Eagle Unbowed*, which quotes a Russian schoolbook from the 1940s describing Glasgow from a somewhat biased Communist point of view. It stated: "The population consists of 95% exploited proletarians and 5% bloodsucker bourgeois. Every evening the bourgeois drive in their limousines, bespattering with mud the proletarians who look for the leavings of food in the gutters and dustbins."

Remarks Howard: "Certainly brings back memories of growing up in Bearsden."

THE SCOTTISH Government's Rural Affairs Secretary, Richard Lochhead, announced a £1m campaign to bolster the Scottish meat business. Alison Campbell tells us that once Scottish stores have been given the all-clear over the horsemeat scandal, the campaign will consist of the Proclaimers singing their new anthem "Co-op nae mare, Asda nae mare, Morrisons nae mare."

THE FINANCIAL world is still arguing over whether the Royal Bank of Scotland should be rejigged into two separate banks. As a financial wizard explained it to us: "They will split RBS into two banks. One that takes your money, and the other that loses it."

FOLK are still talking about the new president of Iran, Hasan Rowhani, getting his PhD from Glasgow Caledonian University.

As Bruce Skivington tells us: "The new president, with his Scottish education, should be able to tell the difference between Iran and Glasgow – one is a society divided by religious intolerance, run by dodgy politicians and with areas of poverty.

"And the other is in the Middle East."

THE TRADES unions' May Day celebrations in Glasgow took place with a May Day Cabaret in Oran Mor featuring among the acts "Marxist magician Ian Saville."

We asked the organisers what a Marxist magician was and were told: "Well, whereas David Copperfield is content with little tricks like making the Statue of Liberty disappear, Ian aims at the much more ambitious goal of making international capitalism and exploitation disappear – although he hasn't entirely succeeded yet."

READER Bob Gardner wades into the independence debate – less than 500 days to go, folks – to claim: "In a survey about Scottish independence, 1,000 folk in Paisley were asked if they thought the currency should change. Almost all of them said no – they were happy with the giro."

IT WAS REPORTED that the police had to race Prime Minister David Cameron's passport to the airport when he went on holiday as he had left it behind in Downing Street.

An old buffer at an Ayrshire golf course commented: "He probably thought everywhere else was like Britain where you don't seem to need a passport to get in."

UKIP leader Nigel Farage got all hot and bothered when his trip to Edinburgh ended with him being hounded by protesters in a bar.

Best gag about it came from Gordon Darroch who said: "Nigel Farage walks into a bar, buys a pint and pays with a £20 note. The barman asks, 'Have you got anything smaller?' so Farage gives him a piece of his mind."

FORMER Cabinet minister Chris Huhne was freed after serving two months of an eight-month sentence. "No wonder a week is a long time in politics," a reader phoned to tell us. "As it's the same as four weeks for ordinary people."

POLITICS, and a reader phones to tell us: "Disgraced MP Chris Huhne says he wishes he could turn the clock back. Just how many motoring offences does he want to be found guilty of?"

WE MENTIONED former Clyde shipyard worker Bob Starrett's book *The Way I See It*. In it he tells of the UCS work-in leaders meeting then Prime Minister Ted Heath at 10 Downing Street in their bid to save the yards. Mr Heath, trying to explain the competing problems he had to deal with, asked them: "Do you know the worries I have?" William 'Bugsy' McGuiness retorted: "Worries? You think you've got worries? I support Partick Thistle."

JUNIOR Health Minister at Westminster Anna Soubry says smoking in cars should be banned to protect children. As one smoker who drives his kids to school tells us: "I've decided not to smoke with the kids in the car. The walk will do them good."

ON THE 10th anniversary of the start of the Iraq war, a Scot who was out there tells us of the difference he noticed between American and British troops. "A US Marines armoured column which went past had its vehicles nicknamed 'Lifetaker', 'Soul Stealer' and so on. A bunch of Black Watch squaddies watching them were a bit bemused. Their Warrior fighting vehicle had 'Big Hamish' stencilled on the side."

MINISTER for Work and Pensions Iain Duncan Smith, one of the many millionaires in the Cabinet, has provoked outrage by saying he could live on £53 a week benefits. It reminds a reader of the story about Tony Blair when on the speaking circuit, going into his bank and asking if he could have the amount he could withdraw from the bank's ATMs increased.

"Let's see," said the cashier, "Do you earn more than £25,000?" "It depends," replied Tony. "Some days I do, some days I don't."

AND A COMMENT, not so much on the late Prime Minister but on the education system. Donnie Pollock in Glasgow heard a young chap at his work discussing the funeral and asking: "Baroness Thatcher – was that her real name? Where did she get 'Maggie' from? Why are you all laughing?"

GOOD to see a politician with a sense of humour. A reader was at a charity Burns supper in the west of Scotland where one of the speakers, an SNP MSP, got the biggest laugh when he told the audience he had just read party leader Alex Salmond's autobiography.

It's entitled, he said, *Famous People Who Have Met Me*.

THE FREEZING weather provokes the seasonal gag: "A Scot visiting London slipped and fell just outside Downing Street, and was helped to his feet by David Cameron.

"'Thanks,' said the Scot politely. 'If you really want to thank me,' joked the Prime Minister, 'just vote for my party at the next election.' 'Listen, pal,' said the Scot. 'I landed on my backside, no' ma heid.'"

BURNS NIGHT, and giving the Toast to the Lassies at the Glasgow Lord Provost's Burns Supper was the council's deputy leader Archie Graham, who is married to Labour's Scottish leader Johann Lamont. Archie, in a robust description of his marriage, claimed he once got the condolences of First Minister Alex Salmond as "you've got to listen to that every day of the week."

After adding that when he worked in the building trade and was given two sets of ear defenders – one set for the site, and one for when he got home, Lord Provost Sadie Docherty reassured Archie he could sleep on her settee that night if he got kicked out.

HOWEVER Johann, in giving the Reply From the Lassies, gave as good as she got, telling everyone: "When I met Archie, he boasted he could do the work of two men. He didn't tell me they were Laurel and Hardy."

AT the Edinburgh Fringe, Scots comedian Vladimir McTavish has not been impressed by politicians claiming that Britain's Olympic successes will strengthen the Union vote in Scotland's independence referendum.

As Vladimir told the audience at his show *Look at the State of Scotland*: "Will people go into the polling stations thinking, 'This is the most important day in 300 years of our nation's history, but I was still more moved by Mr Bean falling asleep at the piano two years ago.'"

THE PRO-UNION campaign Better Together being nicknamed Bitter Together reminds David Macleod in Lenzie of a visit to the Philips factory in Hamilton by the company's top brass from Europe. Waiting to greet them was the company logo, Let's Make Things Better, in 6ft-high letters at the factory entrance.

Unfortunately nobody had noticed that some wag had changed the order of the words so that it read Let's Make Better Things.

14
Watch Your Feet

Even encounters with the police can raise a smile.

RETIRED traffic cop Willie Bennie tells us of the speeding driver stopped on Glasgow's Great Western Road who was asked to sit in the back of the police car, and as it was a very wet day, one officer told him: "Watch your feet in that puddle."

A few days later the officers were summoned by their chief inspector who said that he had received a complaint from a driver who accepted that he was speeding, but what he did object to was being told to wash his feet in a puddle before getting into the police car.

GLASGOW buses can be very sociable places. Jim Campbell from Stepps was on a local bus when a police car stopped in front of the vehicle. Two officers got out, boarded the bus and went upstairs. Says Jim: "They came down with a male passenger in tow, at which point another man called out, 'Hey Jimmy, do you want me to tell yer ma?'"

A VIGNETTE of Scottish football at the weekend where a reader heard a football fan discussing his trip to an away game in the SPL, and how he managed to cadge a lift back on a supporters' bus.

"So they had a spare seat?" asked his pal.

"Aye," the chap replied. "It was full originally, but fortunately someone got lifted."

RUSSELL MARTIN in Bearsden recalls being stopped speeding in his sports car on the M6 when the police officer taking his details charitably suggested he might check his mirror more often so that he would be less likely to be caught.

Says Russell: "I was tempted to reply that, driving at that speed, would it not be better to look where I was going and not where I'd been, but thought probably best not to."

A SMALL quantity of drugs was found by police on board the tour bus of teenage pop star Justin Bieber. Paddy Power immediately opened a book on what the drugs are. You can bet on Calpol at 100/1.

OUR TALE of what to say to police officers when they stop you leads to reader Jim Hair claiming one woman who was stopped told the officer she believed 40 was the new 30.

THE STORY about the police stopping a chap in Glasgow with his baby under his jacket reminds a reader of being in the city centre when two officers threatened a rowdy drunk with being locked up for the night if he didn't behave.

"What's the charge?" shouted the aggressive drunk.

It went over his head when one officer replied: "Oh there's no charge. It's a free service."

OUR TALE of the restaurant's phone number being mixed up with the hospital number, reminds Phylis Anderson in Milton of Campsie: "I called, as I thought, a local shop one Friday to have groceries delivered.

"Because of one digit being incorrect, I rang the local police station by mistake and asked for a delivery.

"'Whit dae ye fancy? A couple o' drunks? Plenty to spare on a Friday night,' replied the officer who answered."

A READER at an Ayrshire golf club tells us the discussion in the club bar was the old argument about prisoners getting too soft a regime these days. While the old arguments were trotted out, our reader thought one golfer came up with a new line when he announced: "I saw a prisoner being taken to court last week, and because it was cold he had an electric blanket over his head."

THE CHRIS HUHNE speeding case reminds David Speedie in New York of being stopped in Maryland by a state trooper for speeding, and David remonstrating: "But officer, there were other cars going at least as fast as I was."

The officer replied: "You know, ah go out duck huntin'. Ah see a string of ducks up there, ah aim and fire. One duck comes down, the rest keep on flyin'.""

"No real answer to that," says David.

HUGH WALSH in Dalry, Ayrshire, was so concerned about stories of pet dogs being stolen in the area he decided to take a walking stick with him when out with his dog in case he needed a deterrent.

Says Hugh: "Along the way I called in at the local baker, tied the dog outside and left the stick against the wall. On leaving the shop I found the dog safe, but the stick had gone."

A GLASGOW reader tells us about his optimistic pal who was stopped by the police for speeding. The officer came over to his car and asked: "Do you know why you were stopped?" His friend came out with the hopeful, yet misguided, reply: "Are you possibly looking for directions?"

A CHAP was stopped by cops in Govan walking away from the Southern General hospital with a large sign under his arm which read: "And Emergency". When they asked him where he got it, he told them he found it by accident.

BIG DAY at Wimbledon for Andy Murray. It reminds Bill Heaney of nipping into a butcher's shop in Edinburgh which had parking restrictions on the road outside.

The butcher reassured Bill by telling him: "Traffic wardens around here are like tennis players – they don't come out when it's raining."

A CHAP in a Glasgow bar at the weekend announced his wife had got a job with the Parole Board. When his pals expressed surprise at the announcement, he added: "She was a natural for it as she never lets anyone finish a sentence."

TELEVISION subtitling continues to throw up the occasional oddity. Says John Neil Munro: "Was just watching the BBC's *Reporting Scotland* news bulletin. They had an item on the campaign against the proposed court closures in Scotland. The subtitles got the story a bit wrong – instead of the campaign being vociferous, it was 'for syphilis.'"

MISTAKING names continued. Stephen Gold was told some years ago by the then president of the Scottish Law Society, Norman Biggart, a very distinguished lawyer of his day, that the high point of his term of office was receiving a fraternal letter from the President of the American Bar Association, addressed to Norman Bigfart.

A GLASGOW primary teacher tells us she took her class to the local park as a nature trip, where she told them not to pick the flowers.

When she then asked them: "And why do we not pick the

flowers?" she expected a reply about letting other people enjoy them, But instead one wee boy put his hand up and told her: "Because the police are always watching you."

DUNDEE author David Aitken, whose new detective novel *A Dundee Detective*, has just been published, wonders if fact is stranger than fiction after he was threatened by two men in a highway underpass while visiting Hong Kong. Suddenly an old woman appeared, chopped one of the potential muggers on the jugular, turning the chap's legs to rubber, and blowing on a whistle which immediately summoned two police officers who grabbed the second mugger.

The old woman then removed her disguise, explained she was actually a young policewoman and added: "I was the one who was supposed to be mugged." David just wonders why they thought he was an easier target.

OUR daft gag last week prompted Jim McCrudden: "Thieves have just robbed my local shop of twenty cases of Red Bull. I don't know how these people sleep at night."

A MILNGAVIE reader tells us he had occasion to visit a lawyer, and while he was there he said he thought it was perhaps time he had a will drawn up. "Yes, leave it all to me," said the lawyer who added: "Sorry, I tell that joke to everyone who comes in wanting a will."

ORGANISATIONS are now using the social network site Twitter – some with a bit more deftness than others. Foster Evans likes a recent tweet by Solihull Police which stated: "Anyone lost a huge amount of cannabis in the Chelmsley Wood area? Don't panic, we found it. Please come to the police station to collect it."

TALKING about Twitter, Solihull Police also gave the excellent advice: "Sing like no-one is listening, dance like no one is watching, tweet – only what you're happy to have read out in court!"

15
Where The Roundabouts Come From

Scots can even turn their poor beginnings into a gag.

CAR manufacturer Vauxhall is advertising that any new car bought this week will qualify for £500 worth of petrol. "Or enough to get you home, then," says a reader.

THIS CONFIRMS what we've always suspected about Scotland's new towns. In the foreword to the just published *Livingston Lives* by archivist Emma Peattie, retired local GP Frank Stewart writes: "There is a tale told about the planning of Livingston new town that whenever the designers stopped for a cup of coffee, a round mark appeared on the road plan and a corresponding roundabout duly appeared on the ground."

"I OFFERED the pensioner next door a fiver to have a shot on her Stannah stair-lift," a reader phones to tell us. "I think she's going to take me up on it . . ."

JOHN PARK in Motherwell tells us: "The colder temperatures this week remind me of the depth of last year's winter when a wife texted her husband at work to tell him, 'Windows frozen.'"

Knowing what to do with your car on a frosty morning, he texted back, "Pour some lukewarm water over it." Half an hour later she texted, "Computer completely knackered now."

GREAT to see British photographer Craig Easton, who now works around the world, has been named Travel Photographer of the Year. His stunning winning portfolio is named *Dreich*, and yes, you've guessed it, was entirely snapped in Scotland.

OUR LANGUAGE is usually a beautiful communications tool. However, a reader was in a Motherwell social work office where the queuing system involves taking a printed number from a machine and waiting for it to come up on a screen. A Polish chap was looking puzzled, so a local woman shouted over to help: "You've got to thingy the thing." This somehow didn't help the chap, so she tried again, with more vehemence: "Thingy the thing!" at this our reader stepped in to help, despite the woman's obviously clear instructions.

A READER admits he couldn't stop laughing when his wife during a particularly hectic spell at home announced: "I am running about here like a blue-a**** chicken."

DO CATS rule the house? A Bearsden reader tells us she adopted a stray cat which has now started to use the back of the sofa as a scratching post.

Her husband said he would teach the cat to stop doing that by immediately putting it outside when it touched the sofa.

Adds our reader: "Ever since, when the cat wants to go outside it simply scratches the back of the sofa."

A READER swears to us the young chap on his bus into Glasgow yesterday told his pal: "My next-door neighbour banged on my door at two in the morning claiming he couldn't sleep. I told him he was in luck as I was having a party and he should just come in."

NOT QUITE overheard – Mark Johnston tells us about a friend who was voted Best Dressed Man at a local fundraising event. Says Mark: "He went on to say that the MC had referred to him as 'the rakish pinnacle of sartorial elegance – our very own Don Juan.'

"Unfortunately, his wife then burst his bubble by laughing hysterically and saying: 'You need your hearing checked. He said Gok Wan, not Don Juan.'"

MUNGO HENNING was in a discussion about how cold houses were before central heating when one chap upped the ante by declaring he could remember winters so cold that ice formed on the inside of glass windows.

Says Mungo: "His bubble was burst when someone countered his claim with the remark: 'Lucky so-and-so had glass.'"

POVERTY bragging continued. says Jim McCrudden: "Our house was so damp that when the sun shone into the bedroom there was a rainbow over my bed."

JIM SCOTT tells us: "I always remember sports broadcaster Chick Young's comment, 'The area I grew up in was so poor even the advent calendar had bars on the windows.'"

BRAGGING about poverty continued. Phil McCluskey tells us: "The biggest leathering I ever got as a child was when I had been in the butcher's with my mother and she asked him for a bone for the dog.

I immediately called out: 'Mum, are we getting a dog?'"

WE MUST draw our poverty bragging to a close, but not before a Motherwell reader declared: "We were so poor we had to eat scraps for our tea.

"I still miss that dog."

WE HAVE mentioned a few working-class tales, but what about the middle classes? John Gerrard in Arizona boasts: "We were so poor growing up in Giffnock, we could only give the gardener plain digestive biscuits with his morning cuppa."

THE STORY about the nature reserve staff putting flags in the ground beside dog poo reminds a reader: "I once heard a woman in Glasgow talking about a shy chap to a friend. She used a far more colourful phrase than she perhaps intended when she told her pal, 'He wouldn't say poo to a goose.'"

AFTER our "wouldn't say poo to a goose" story, Jamie Wilkie in Australia tells us: "My former father-in-law, a keen home baker, would often list defecated coconut as one of the key ingredients in his cakes. Needless to say, I always stayed well clear."

OUR STORY about mistaken names reminds Kenneth Maxwell: "I too was in discussion with a company south of the Border who wished to send me some information. Being north of the Border it was obvious that I must be a MacSwell as this was how I was addressed on the subsequent mailing."

PRONOUNCING names continued. Scott Macintosh tells us: "I was listening to a telesales operator in full swing extolling her products when without any warning she asked for my name. taken by surprise I stumbled, 'Eh, Mr Macintosh.' The samples she subsequently sent out were addressed to Emerson Macintosh."

MALAPROPISMS as Roddie McNicol in Bearsden passes on: "I overheard two ladies on the train discussing their failure to cope with life. One commented that she felt that she had been swept away 'by wan o' they salamis.'"

POVERTY bragging continued. Says Bruce Skivington: "Growing up in Leith we couldn't find out anything because we could never afford to give anyone a penny for their thoughts."

A DISCUSSION on current affairs was taking place in a Glasgow pub at the weekend where one lady declared: "If women ran the world, there wouldn't be any wars." "Maybe," piped up a chap who was listening, "but there would be entire nations that weren't speaking to each other."

DURING SOME brief good weather in Glasgow, regulars in a pub were talking about going for a walk in the public parks, but how a lone male walking in a park often got some strange looks.

"I blend in," replied one of the topers, "by always carrying a plastic bag of dog poo with me."

A READER tells us he bought his mum a commemorative Prince Charles teapot off eBay because she is such an enthusiast for the Royal Family. Now whenever she uses it, she tells guests she likes the teapot because "it never reigns, but it pours."

TWO WOMEN were discussing a mutual friend in a Glasgow coffee shop when one of them came up with the description: "She's so lazy she's even got a snooze button on her smoke alarm."

POPE BENEDICT'S resignation came only weeks after he had opened an account on the social media network Twitter. As one businessman told us yesterday: "The Pope is not the first person to lose interest in their real job as soon as they get obsessed with Twitter."

BRITISH troops stationed in Germany are being brought home. We remember a former soldier telling us that he had reported a broken towel rail in his married quarters in Germany and, losing patience while waiting for the repair, he bought a new rail and put it up.

Weeks later someone eventually arrived to replace the broken one, but when he pointed out he had done it himself, the chap replied: "Says right here on my work order, replace towel rail," which he then proceeded to do, taking off the new one.

Near Yzeures-sur Creuse,
24/05/2013

POST CRUFTS, we asked for your dog stories, and naturally Andy Cameron told us: "I once had a Rottweiler and a Dachshund, and one day after a heavy fall of snow I took them for a walk and discovered they could speak.

"As we trudged through the snow the Rottweiler complained, 'Ma paws are freezing.'

"The wee Dachshund gave him a look of disdain and said, 'Your paws are freezing?'"

IT'S WORLD Plumbing Day – unless of course it doesn't arrive, in which case you phone up and it's rearranged for a week on Tuesday.

It reminds us of the doctor who phoned the local plumber to complain about his toilet being blocked, and insisted that the plumber come out that very evening.

So the plumber arrived, threw two aspirin tablets into the toilet and told the doc: "If it's still blocked in the morning, phone my office."

MORE CRUFTS stories as Iain Gifford in Inverurie recalls: "My wife once bought raffle tickets and, as you do, put different family members' names on each one, including Judy, our dog. As luck would have it, Judy's number came up and she won £50. The problem came when my wife went to pay the cheque into the bank, and the teller had to be convinced that Judy was indeed a family member.

"My wife used some of the money to buy the dog a new basket. I thought she was daft even to have told Judy she was a winner."

CHRISTMAS present buying, and many folk are thinking of getting their ageing parents computers. One Jordanhill reader tells us he got one for his mum last year, showed her Google and said you could put in any question you wanted.

His mum then typed: "How's Aunty Helen keeping?"

TWITTER may seem new but last week it celebrated its seventh anniversary. As a reader told us: "How time flies when you're wasting it."

CONCERN in the queue at Auchterarder Post Office where customers notice that a member of staff had scrawled "F Off" across the office calendar behind the desk. Had someone succumbed to the pressures of the job? Eventually a customer asked what was going on, and was relieved to hear that Fiona had merely marked down an upcoming holiday.

A GROUP of women were discussing various ways of self-improvement in a Glasgow coffee shop when one of them declared: "I go to a book club with the girls after work on Friday. So far we only read wine labels, but it's a start."

THE DUKE OF YORK abseiled down the Shard skyscraper building for charity yesterday. Many a reader wondered if when he was only halfway up, he felt he was neither up nor down.

TALES of pianos remind Michael Grace of BBC Radio Highland running a swap shop for listeners' unwanted items, and a woman from Dingwall phoning to swap a piano. He still remembers the broadcaster asking: "Is it a grand piano, Betty?" and Betty replying: "Oh aye, it's a topper."

HERALD crossword solvers were fearing a lurch to the demotic last week when the clue "Rush of air from wife's behind" was a four-letter word which was something a, something t. Says Ian Duff in Inverness: "My good lady was so shocked I had to fold the paper and revive her by wafting it around to cool her down. Oh, wait a minute. Waft. Oh thank goodness for that."

STORIES of spelling difficulties remind Yvonne Mitchell of, in her younger days, hesitating when having to write a cheque for £30 as she suddenly was unsure how to spell thirty. Her solution? She handed over three cheques for £10 each.

OUR STORIES about spelling difficulties remind a retired police officer in Ayr: "While carrying out speed detection checks in deepest

Ayrshire along with a colleague many years ago, an offender was detected and gave his occupation as an anaesthetist. After sending the driver on his way and checking the speeding ticket I saw my colleague had written the occupation as 'gas doctor'."

THE STORY of the woman who wrote that her son played the banjo as she couldn't spell ukulele reminds Bill Wright in Glasgow, who runs a transport company, of one of his drivers filling in an accident report form after a collision with a trailer transporting a large yacht.

Says Bill: "He had various attempts at spelling yacht, before eventually giving up and drawing a picture of a boat complete with sail."

READER Bernard Gray was driving behind a tanker operated by the Hamilton firm of Grant Henderson when he idly wondered what cargo it was carrying. Then he noticed on the side of the tanker, the company's website – www.wemovesh.it – and wondered why a Hamilton company would have an Italian website.

SIR Walter Scott's hefty *Ivanhoe* novel has been edited to half its size by Professor David Purdie to make it more accessible to new readers. As ex-surgeon Prof Purdie put it at the novel's launch by Scottish publishers Luath Press: "I removed more colons than in a lifetime of abdominal surgery."

16
Did You Take Anything

As the Reader's Digest has been saying for years, laughter is the best medicine.

YOU CAN even find Glasgow humour in the city's accident and emergency units. A reader waiting at the Southern General watched as an elderly woman was being brought in on an ambulance trolley, and her condition was being discussed by medical staff.

As a paramedic explained: "BP is 127" our reader was told by the chap sitting next to him: "Imagine them discussing petrol prices at a time like that."

A GLASGOW pharmacist swears to us that a senior citizen came in for advice about a spot of constipation that had been troubling her. She said that for the past week, no matter how long she sat in the bathroom, nothing was happening.

"Did you take anything?" asked the pharmacist.

"Well, I took a magazine," replied the puzzled lady.

THE TALE of the old golfer worried about dying reminds a reader of the poster in the waiting room at the Queen Mum's maternity hospital in Glasgow.

He tells us: "It read, 'Have faith, the first few minutes of life are the most dangerous.'

"Someone had added the graffiti, 'The last few are no' too clever either.'"

TALKING of health, Andrew Foster, visiting from Canada, was on the train from Oban to Glasgow when two chaps were in a desperate hurry to get past the refreshment trolley in order to get to the toilet.

Says Andrew: "After some shuffling and shunting the Glesga wummin in charge of the trolley managed to let them past, interrupting her sales patter just long enough to announce to everyone in the carriage, 'Thae men – their prostates are a' gone!' and carried on selling coffee and sandwiches.

"I sat with my legs tightly crossed until we got to Glasgow."

THE EATING habits of Scots continued. David Macleod in Lenzie said a colleague at work told him there was a new warning sign put up in the staff canteen. When David asked what it was, the chap replied: "Salad bar."

DOUGIE MCNICOL was in a Bridge of Weir pub where one imbiber revealed: "When the doc asked me about alcohol I told him I hadn't touched a drop for eighteen years. He was very impressed." After a long gulp of his pint, he added: "So I didn't want to spoil it by saying that since my eighteenth birthday I've hardly stopped."

RETIREMENT can mean quite a life change for many people. A senior citizen from the south side of Glasgow tells us the talk at the bowling club the other day was what time did retirees go to bed, now that they no longer had to get up for their work in the morning.

One chap explained his regime by telling them: "My bedtime is three hours after I fall asleep on the couch."

ANDY CUMMING was on holiday in York when he heard a large chap at the next table ordering breakfast and asking for an extra sausage, bacon, black pudding, one more egg and a drop of beans. The waitress reads back the order: "For the lady, porridge. And two cooked breakfasts for sir."

ONE-THIRD of men in a recent survey admitted to having a mid-life crisis, many of whom splashed out on sports cars or motorbikes. A reader tells us he attended the fiftieth birthday party of a friend who had treated himself to a large, fast motorbike. At the party another pal told the birthday boy: "We clubbed together to get you what we thought would be the most appropriate gift," and handed him an organ donor card.

A DUNBARTONSHIRE reader tells us he went for a haircut last week when there was a discount for pensioners. He realised he had no proof of age on him, but the barber told him: "That won't be necessary."

"Do I have an honest face?" asked our reader.

"No, you're just very old-looking," replied the chap with the scissors.

GLASWEGIANS sometimes have a strange type of pessimism. This was shown to a reader visiting a friend in the Western Infirmary who heard an elderly woman in the lift behind him tell her companion: "But then again Margaret, if they cure him he'll no' have anything to moan about."

A READER on a bus into Glasgow heard an old biddy tell her pal that she had just finished a course of antibiotics.

When the friend asked what was wrong with her, the surprising answer was: "Nothing. But ma' husband hadn't finished his antibiotics – and ye cannae' let good antibiotics go to waste."

A NURSE at Glasgow's Southern General tells us she was explaining to a recovering heart patient that his future health regime should include activity three times a week which got his heart beating faster. "Like shoplifting?" he asked.

A READER having his shower room fixed was told by the chap from Clean Tile and Grout Scotland that an elderly gentleman had come up to its stall at the Ideal Home Show in Glasgow and asked if the firm could help with a fungal infection.

When the company rep asked where it was, the chap said it was in his left toe. Confusion all round until the elderly chap pointed at their sign and said: "Oh, I'm sorry I thought it said gout."

MIKE RITCHIE was visiting a chemist's in the south side of town when he noticed two scrapers on the counter, and he wondered what ailment would require the use of such painful-looking implements.

So he was relieved when he tentatively asked what they were for and was told: "We use them for removing chewing gum that customers drop on the floor."

FOLK have different ways of fundraising for charity. Hugh Campbell in the Highlands says his local dentist was using a novel way last week. Says Hugh: "He would ask patients, already flat-out in the chair, 'now then! Would you prefer a blunt needle, or a nice sharp needle and a book of raffle tickets?'"

DONALD GRANT in Paisley heard a senior chap at the golf club announce he had consumed his five a day before leaving the house that day.

A fellow golfer asked if he was on a health kick, but the chap replied: "Pills: statin, warfarin, prostate, beta-blockers and now hayfever."

VEGETARIANISM is still tricky for folk in Glasgow to get to grips with.

A reader swears to us he was in a city-centre shop buying his lunchtime sandwich when a young girl asked the shop assistant: "Are you sure these are vegetarian? It says beef tomatoes on the package."

A WOMAN in a Glasgow coffee shop was heard telling her friend that she went to see her doctor about a back pain, and he recommended she see a chiropractor.

"I swear for a few seconds I thought he was wanting to send me to Egypt," she added.

We reckon it's the fault of Egypt being in the news so much these days.

WE WISH the Queen a quick recovery from her bout of ill health. As one reader phones to tells us: "It must be strange for the Queen to be in a hospital that doesn't smell of fresh paint."

A SOUTH side chap was telling his pals he had recently been in a private hospital having an ankle injury treated. He added: "The surgeon said I would be up and walking in two weeks. He was right – I had to sell my car, the hospital bill was that high."

A PARTICK reader confesses to us that he is starting a diet right away after ordering a carry-out from his local Indian restaurant. When he unpacked the food he noticed the restaurant had included two sets of plastic cutlery rather than one.

OUR PAISLEY bus story reminded Alan Barlow: "I was on the bus to the Royal Alexandra Hospital and a couple of stops before the hospital a chap ran out of a shop clutching a roll and sausage and jumped on the bus.

"Nothing unusual about that except he was wearing pyjamas and slippers.

"As he disappeared into the hospital at journey's end two things struck me – his resilience and the quality of hospital food."

GROWING old has frequently been discussed in the Diary. Donald Grant in Paisley comments: "Talking with friends recently we got round to what we did first thing in the morning before opening our eyes. "An indication to our age may be that one said the first thing he did was to stretch out his arms – and sigh with relief when his hands didn't touch wood."

GUS FURRIE in East Kilbride tells us his wife was visiting Hair-myres Hospital's accident and emergency department when she overheard the woman in the next cubical telling the doctor that she couldn't open her eyes because the pain was so terrible. Eventually after a discussion about the type of pain, the doctor carried out some treatment, and the woman eventually declared: "Oh doctor that's fantastic, I can open my eyes . . . oh no will you look at how he has dressed me!"

WILL the poor folk at Tesco never be forgiven? A reader tells us: "Seen leaving Lochgilphead last Saturday – the white, articulated Tesco delivery truck with the additional text, graffiti style, along the length of the trailer, hand-written in the traffic grime: "Caution – horses in transit."

EVEN football fans are becoming more health conscious. A reader attending St Mirren's thrashing of Ayr United in the league cup heard a bored Ayr United fan who had taken out a Weight Watcher's points card, excitedly exclaim: "Bovril's only one point!"

GLASGOW consultant John Larkin's book, *How To Keep Your Doctor Happy* urges patients to be more specific when talking to their docs, and gives as a bad example a discussion which went: "And the last time you had the chest pain was?"

"A year ago."

"And what were you doing at the time?"

"I was an architect."

SPELLING problems continued. Pat Reid in Falkirk tells us: "As a manager, I once received a sickness certificate note from an employee who had been off work for a couple of days with an upset stomach.

"After four abortive attempts to spell diarrhoea, all of which had been scored out, he had resorted with a flourish to the word 'skitters.'"

17
That's A Famous Name

With the Scottish weather, no wonder a holiday abroad puts a smile on many folks' lips.

THE SHOCKING spring weather in Scotland has sent many folk to travel agents booking summer holidays in the sun. A reader was in one Glasgow travel shop where a couple of young girls were trying to book a flight to Spain that their pals were already booked on. Looking up from his terminal, the travel agent told them: "I'm sorry, there's no seats left on that flight." "Do we have to stand?" asked one of the girls.

BURNS NIGHT reminds an East Kilbride reader of getting in a cab in New York and noticing from the driver's licence that his name was Robert Burns.

Making conversation, our reader said to him: "That's a famous name you have."

"It should be," the chap replied. "I've been driving a cab here for nearly forty years."

LOOKING forward to your summer holidays? A reader suggests a fun way to spend the time on your holiday plane. "Find out," he tells us, "how loud your partner can scream by waking them up on the flight while wearing your life jacket and oxygen mask."

ELECTION time in America, and a Bearsden businessman contacts us from the States where he passed a line of folk waiting to vote. In the queue were a couple in their forties and their son aged about twenty who seemed unhappy.

"You weren't complaining when you had to wait to buy an iPhone," his mum calmly told him.

MORE on Americans. Kate Woods recalls living on the outskirts of New Orleans some years ago. She looked out of the window to see a goat grazing in the garden.

Says Kate: "I chased it away before it could do any more damage to my flower beds.

"A short while later a neighbour rang the doorbell and said, 'I know that you come from a foreign country so I thought that I should let you know that the animal in your yard this morning is called a goat and is relatively harmless'.

"I thanked him kindly."

"I GOT an email from a hotel company saying if I booked a holiday then my kids could go free," said the chap in a Glasgow pub the other night. "Things must be bad if they've turned to kidnapping," he added.

GLASGOW Council, seeking a new slogan for the city, asked for people's favourite stories about Glasgow, and a chap called Lachie wrote: "Visiting with my brother from Australia we came across the old fruit market and wandered in for a look.

"The guard hailed to us that he was closing the building. We replied that we were just wandering around reminiscing.

"He nodded his approval and we wandered on. After about 500 metres he called to us, 'What does reminiscing mean?'"

A PENSIONER catching the bus to Glasgow from Oban announced to everyone on board: "I wish I was as attractive to women as I am to midges."

GRAHAM BACON in Dunblane, tells us how youngsters can fair embarrass you at times. A friend took her four-year-old daughter to an open day at a posh country house in the Borders where they were having tea on the lawn amid some women with big hats.

The young girl asked to go to the loo, but the mum asked her to hold on until later as there were no loos around.

The young girl tried to be helpful by saying she could just pee on the grass. This was also hurriedly refused until the little one made heads turn by loudly declaring: "But you always let me pee on the grass at home, mummy."

CATCHING a ferry to the continent reminds Ian Glasgow: "I once saw a magician on a ferry where the crowd was also a bit uninterested. He managed to persuade a volunteer to go up on stage and blindfold him.

"But after doing this the volunteer just walked off stage never to be seen again, leaving the magician asking thin air to 'Pick a card'. It was funnier than the comedian."

ALSO on holiday was the Scot in a Spanish hotel complex who was watching the Brazil v Italy Confederation Cup game on the telly and trying to decipher as much as he could from the Spanish commentary.

"Just like watching the fitba on BBC Alba," a fellow Scot at the bar commented.

EDINBURGH Bus Tours marked World Heritage Day by inaugurating a new Edinburgh World Heritage Tour, which covers more sites than previous tours. One of the guides at the company tells us that, on one of the earlier tours, there was a particularly thick haar which obscured the castle. So he merely pointed towards it and joked: "That's where Edinburgh Castle used to be."

Unfortunately one of the tourists on board asked: "What happened to it?" He realised he only confused matters more by replying: "It's away to be cleaned."

AMERICANS continued. Ian Cooper in Bearsden was decorating his house while his wife was visiting friends in Houston, Texas. When she phoned he told her that he had struck his little finger with a hammer. Says Ian: "She returned to the dinner table and announced that I had whacked myself on the pinky with a claw hammer as a result of which it was badly bruised and had had to be bandaged. This was greeted by a ghastly silence on the part of the other guests, which mystified her, until her hostess quietly advised her that in that part of the world a man's pinky was not positioned on his hand at all but in a delicate position elsewhere."

THE STORY of the French fashion store offering Bellshill T-shirts reminds John Daly in Houston of being in Paris to see France play Scotland at football, where he saw one Scotsman wearing a T-shirt with "ventilateur" printed on the back.

The poor chap had no doubt used an electronic dictionary to find out the French for fan and have it printed as a welcoming gesture. Alas ventilateur is of the electric fan variety.

AIRPORT security: It's still tricky trying to work out whether you take your shoes and your belt off. A reader on business in Chicago heard an announcement over the Tannoy: "Will the gentleman with his pants at his ankles please return to security and retrieve your belt."

A READER in Texas tells us that the senior vice-president appointed to a local investment company, the Sterling Group, is a Jim Apple. In a whimsical way, our reader ponders: "Do you think it's confusing when he tries to book a room in France?"

MOVING story of Terry Waite going back to Lebanon where he was held captive by terrorists for five years. Graeme Liveston in Milngavie tells us the television interview with Waite was spoiled slightly when the interviewer's question: "It must have been very emotional for you returning to Lebanon and walking through the same streets", was put in the subtitles as: "And walking through Sainsbury's."

AN EDINBURGH reader visiting her son in Australia had gone over for the birth of her grandson, and tells us that when she went to the maternity hospital to visit her daughter-in-law, someone had neatly added in pen on the door where it said Push the additional words "Push! Push!"

"I DIDN'T expect the BBC to describe the rebels in Mali as toe-rags," said the chap on the bus into Glasgow yesterday. "I think you'll find it's Touaregs," said his pal. "Not quite the same thing."

AS ITHERS see us. Well if Scots can still joke about the alleged financial canniness of fellow Scots, who can blame foreigners from joining in? A reader in the US sends us a cutting from his local newspaper's fun page which states: "Wee Jock has been crying all day because his hamster died. 'Ye didnae cry like that when yer Granny died,' says his mother.

"'Aye, but I didnae pay fer her wi' ma poacket money.'"

A GLASGOW reader back from a beach holiday in the Caribbean tells us his sons amused themselves by trying to catch the names of girls on holiday with their boyfriends walking past on the beach.

If her name was, say, Anita they would write "Marry Me Anita" in big letters on the sand then watch the reaction when the couple walked back past them.

AS ITHERS see us. A reader in the US sends us this from his local newspaper: "Winters are fierce in Northern Scotland, so the owner of the estate felt he was doing a good deed when he bought a pair of earmuffs for his foreman. One cold, blustery day, he noticed that the foreman wasn't wearing them.

"He asked, 'Didn't you like the earmuffs?' 'Oh, they kept my ears nice and toasty warm. But on the first cold day, someone offered to buy me a drink, and, God forbid – I didn't hear him.'"

GERMAN President Angela Merkel's controversial visit to Greece allows Stephen Gold to update an old gag by telling us the news from Athens was that when Mrs Merkel arrived in Greece she was asked her nationality by an officious border guard. When she replied: "German" he then asked "Occupation?" She replied: "Not this time, we're only here for the day."

18
Keeping Fit

Well done, those who can even make fun of sweaty, sore, heart-pumping keep-fit sessions.

KEEPING fit is on many minds in January. "I went out for a run at the weekend," said a chap in a Glasgow bar to his pals. "But had to go back after two minutes because I'd forgotten something."

When a mate asked what, he added: "I'd forgotten I'm fat, unfit and can't run for more than two minutes."

AN EDINBURGH reader was in a city coffee shop when a young woman with her friends suddenly let her face crumble as she told them: "Oh no, I forgot to update my Facebook status saying I was at the gym." "What a waste of a workout."

A WEST-END reader was taking her bicycle on the train to Stirling and asked for a return ticket from Queen Street. "Why don't I just give you a single," said the ticket seller trying to be encouraging. "It's only twenty miles. You could manage that."

GLASGOW'S streets are packed with joggers, but it wasn't always the case. Author Paul Collicutt's new novel *The Murder Mile* is based on athletics, with the police chief modelled on Steve Ovett's Glasgow-born training partner Matt Paterson.

Says Paul: "Apparently when Matt started running in Glasgow it was so uncool he had to go out in his jeans and a shirt and pretend he was running for the bus if anyone saw him."

PIONEER jogging continued. Says Ian McIntyre from Dumfries: "Years ago when I was out running I spotted friends. Immediately feeling self-conscious, I pulled up the hood on my sweatshirt, put my head down and increased pace.

"I felt some relief in getting some space between me and them, only to suddenly experience anguishing pain to my head. I had run into the tailgate of a stationery lorry, splitting my head open.

"At least my friends were there to pick me up."

JOGGING continued. Paul Cortopassi in Bonnybridge decided to try a little jog between two lamp-posts while en route to the newsagents. Says Paul: "While doing so I was easily overtaken by a bus. Slowing down to a stagger I noticed that the bus had stopped. I realised the driver had noticed this aged pedestrian – in fur hat and muffler – shuffling along and had assumed I was running for his bus.

"I almost got on to save any embarrassment."

SAYS Glen Elliot in Elgin: "When limbering up for my first Glasgow marathon a spectator made the following observation: 'Heh auld yin, the last time I saw legs like that, there wis a message tied tae them.'"

IT'S THAT time of year when folk join health clubs after splurging out at Christmas. A member of a posh health club in Glasgow tells us a new exercise class recently started at the club. One member dubbed it The Euthanasia Society, as every week there were fewer folk attending it.

WE ASKED for stories about jogging in earlier times, and Charles Westwood tells us: "In the 1970s I was out alone for a training run one evening on Maryhill Road. An old lady at a bus stop remarked as I passed, 'You're quite right son – the bus service is terrible.'"

BBC SCOTLAND'S traffic staff warned motorists in February that a large exercise ball was bouncing around on the south-bound carriageway of Glasgow's Kingston Bridge. One of them added the possible explanation: "It's someone who's obviously sick of the New Year exercise regime."

NEW YORK CITY has gone green by introducing hundreds of bikes that locals can now hire then leave at various sites around town.

But has it changed the normal tough New Yorker? Reader David Speedie who lives there tells us: "At 64th and Lexington, near my office, I was ambling along in the 30-odd degree heat and heard a voice behind me growl, 'Move over, a******!' I complied and turned to see a woman in her 70s on one of the new bikes."

JOGGING continued. Says Mary Mair from Cumnock: "Arriving late for our regular run, one of our group quickly whipped off his tracksuit and set off to catch us. When he caught up we noticed he was running in his Y-fronts. Bewilderment followed because he clearly remembered putting his running shorts on.

"They were eventually found inside his tracksuit bottoms in the back of his car."

WE SEE a few folk are on diets just now in order to give themselves a bit of slack, as it were, at Christmas. It reminds John Park in Motherwell: "A woman opens her friend's fridge and finds a picture of a slender, scantily-clad woman. Her pal said she put it in there to remind herself not to over-eat.

"When the woman asked if it worked, her pal replied, 'Yes and no. I've lost 15lbs but my husband has gained 20.'"

BEFORE jogging was popular, Bruce Skivington tells us: "In the 1970s, when working in Havant, one of my colleagues used to go out running every morning. He went into the notorious Leigh Park estate where he was lifted by the police who brought him back for confirmation of ID.

"Their explanation was that if they saw someone running at that time of the morning in that area they lifted them and waited for the crime to be discovered."

A READER in Glasgow's west end bumped into friends in the pub back from five-a-side football, and asked how the team was doing. "We've a very promising young player," he was told. "Every week he swears blind he'll turn up, but half the time he doesn't."

19
Television

We ran a whimsical competition where readers changed one letter in a television programme to make a more interesting one.

ONE BORE EVERY MINUTE – Scottish independence opponents put forward their case for the Union. (Frank Bendoris).

LEVIS – an Oxford detective solves who stole the jeans. (Glyn Bragg).

CLOG IT – a game show for teenagers and plumbers. (George Wishart).

COME PINE WITH ME – strangers meet to discuss childhood nostalgic items. (Bill Cassidy).

SASH IN THE ATTIC – about folk who no longer march in July. (Richard Davis).

LUST OF THE SUMMER WINE – chatting up women while on holiday. (Iain McLean).

GORSE – nature show about a jaggy bush. (Richard Gault).

NAME THAT TUBE – Scottish show encouraging viewers to identify petty thieves. (Gary Johnston).

THE TIMPSONS – cartoon family who do shoe repairs and key cutting. (Glyn Bragg).

ONE HORN EVERY MINUTE – documentary about impatient taxi drivers outside the house. (Kevin Mullen).

VASTENDERS – for weightwatchers. (Norman Lawson).

CRIMEWITCH – Kirsty Young cackles round a cauldron while casting spells to trap thieves. (David Belcher).

HOLE TO HOLE – Michael Palin journeys around Scotland. (Richard Gault).

STRICTLY COME LANCING – medieval knockout tournament (Dennis Johnston).

PATCH OF THE DAY – advice show on giving up smoking.

OUTLUMBERED – sitcom about a young man having women trouble.

THE MINGIN DETECTIVE – a Scottish private eye series (Andy Ewan).

HAVE I GOT PEWS FOR YOU – drama of the battle for St George's Tron Church.

ONE FOOT IN THE GRAVY – celebrity cookery show, starring people who can't cook.

LIVER CITY – Scottish soap where characters drink more than is good for them.

COSH IN THE ATTIC – drama about a retired gangster.

FAWLTY TOWELS – comedy set in a badly run laundrette.

AMERICA'S NEXT TOP YODEL – unusual singing contest.

20
Tourists

Scots are always helpful to tourists – but can smile about them at the same time.

WE'VE NOT mentioned American tourists for a while, but George Thorley in Carluke was in Florence the other week marvelling at the gold mosaic ceiling of the 13th-century Baptistery of the Florence Duomo.

Says George: "Behind us sat two Americans who were also marvelling at this breathtaking ceiling. Says the elder to the younger: 'You know kid, this is old stuff. This is really old. We're talking Indiana Jones old.'"

A MAGAZINE article describing Edinburgh as a wasteland reminds Frances Woodward in Yorkshire of seeking directions at the main tourist information office in Edinburgh's Princes Street where she was told to turn right and then it was "downhill all the way".

Says Frances: "There was a slight pause and then she added, 'Metaphorically speaking, of course.'"

A GLASGOW student at Cambridge phones to ask if we are still highlighting the oddities of American tourists. He then adds: "There was one in our local the other day. He said to us, 'So the Boat Race is between Oxford and Cambridge? I've had a look at the map – seems an awful long way.'"

WE MENTIONED Canada Day, which provokes David Macleod in Lenzie to tell us of the two Glasgow guys in the pub who spotted a stranger. One went up to ask where he was from. "Saskatoon, Saskatchewan," the visitor replied.

So the Glasgow chap goes back over to his pal and tells him: "Don't know. He doesn't speak English."

AS ITHERS see us. A visitor to Glasgow who blogs as the Gentle Tourist reported finding a blood trail which led to a teenager slumped against a wall with a bleeding face.

She wrote: "When I asked if he needed help, he declined. Hard to tell exactly what he was saying through strong accent and nasal blood bubbling, but it was along the lines of, 'I deserved it. I've had worse. Careful, don't get blood on your coat.'

"He honestly seemed perfectly cheerful. Glasgow's friendliness is an invaluable asset to a city looking to increase tourism."

So in some ways, quite a positive view of the city.

OUR TALES of Scottish hospitality remind Cristina Cona of a not-to-be-forgotten visit to Lewis, where they ate in a restaurant with surly staff.

Recalls Cristina: "Apart from the service, what really threw us was seeing a large black dog, the same one that had greeted us at the entrance, stroll into the dining room, lift his leg against the wall and relieve himself.

"I must add that nobody intervened to stop him; in fact, nobody even seemed to notice."

BRENDA GILLIES in Newport-on-Tay tells us she was on a flight when the American sitting next to her asked for lemon tea.

The cabin staff replied that there was no fruit tea, just regular.

Says Brenda: "Snorting with derision the young American turned to me and asked, 'Huh, when did lemons become a fruit?'"

OUR TALES of Canadians in Glasgow remind Eric Scott in Australia: "Back when casinos in Glasgow were private clubs which did not admit the local riff-raff, we took the opportunity of being in the company of a Canadian friend to wheedle our way into one of the better-known joints. Signing in with dodgy addresses in Montreal or Ontario we proceeded into the den of sin and fun only to hear our pal, who was still struggling with the visitors' book, call out behind us, 'How do you spell Saskatchewan?'"

AT LAST some great weather. A reader tells us he was surveying the majesty of Stirling Castle with its history, battlements and stunning views when a family arrived with a youngster who suddenly wailed: "I thought you were taking me to a bouncy castle."

A DIARY story reminded Stewart MacKenzie in Newlands of his grandmother visiting from Shrewsbury some years ago and being taken by his Scottish grandmother on the annual women's guild mystery bus tour. Says Stewart: "Desperate for a ciggy, she was delighted when the driver announced they would soon be stopping for smokies – but was disappointed when they merely stopped at a fish shop in Arbroath."

DOUGLAS McLEOD remembers the distant days when pubs shut at 10pm. Customers could buy drink to take home, but signs behind the bar cautioned: 'No carry-outs after 10 o'clock'.

A friend of Douglas's, accompanied by his aunt and her posh Hampstead companion who were holidaying in Scotland, were in Arran's Corrie hotel for a drink. Hampstead lady's gaze fell on the sign. Blissfully unaware of what it meant, she asked, in all seriousness, "Do people really get that drunk up here?"

YES the tourists are slowly trickling in to Glasgow again. A reader was in a smart city-centre cafe when he heard an American ordering a cup of tea. "English breakfast?" asked the waiter. "No, just the tea," replied the visitor.

RESEARCH shows that the British pub is one reason cited by tourists for visiting the UK. A Glasgow reader was reminded of this when an American lady recently entered the pub he was in and asked the portly barman for a diet Coke. The chap looked on his shelves, brought out a regular Coke and told the woman: "Run out of the diet, but you're on your holidays, so go on, have the full-fat one." He then looked down at his considerable girth and added: "As you can see, I've been on my holidays for a good few years now."

WEST-END bar The Sparkle Horse has a slate behind the bar on which the winning pub quiz team has its winnings chalked up, and then the team members can spend the cash on drinks. This week's winners were the imaginatively named The Partick Swayzes, combining local geography and a late lamented American actor. After a few rounds, the prize money was much reduced so the slate simply read "Partick Swayzes, £3.50."

At that three American tourists came into the bar, spotted the slate and ordered: "Three Partick Swayzes." As the barman tried to think up a cocktail to give them, four regulars piped up that they would also like a Partick Swayze, so if you have any idea what should be in it, let us know.

WORDS that don't mean the same across the Atlantic. Says David Macleod in Lenzie: "When my brother visited from Canada, he remarked to my cousin's girlfriend, who normally wears skirts but on this occasion was wearing trousers, 'I think this is the first time I've seen you with pants on.'"

21
Your Turn For The Stairs

A good Scots word – a gallimaufry of stories.

THE NEWS story about the bull escaping from Edinburgh Zoo reminds John Sword at Glasgow's meat market of a bull escape there when it was eventually cornered in the backcourt of a Gallowgate tenement. After the animal was safely secured, a wee wummin went up to the chap who had put it in the lorry and said: "Are you in charge?" Thinking he was about to get a wee hawf or somesuch from a grateful local he cheerily confirmed he was.

"Well it's my turn furra sterrs – so you can clean up," she said and handed the chap a mop and bucket.

BERT PEATTIE in Kirkcaldy tells us there was a local charity, jocularly named the Amalgamated Society of Spongers, Scroungers and Kindred Trades, which raised money for guide dogs, and one grateful owner even called her dog Asskit after the initials of the society.

She later told them she was stopped in a shop and asked the dog's name. She replied "Asskit" and moments later heard a voice now below her waist level saying: "What's your name?"

THE YARN about the supposed escaped lion in Essex reminds Allan Morrison in Glasgow: "There was a Glasgow veterinary practice which had a large notice outside their premises which stated, 'Veterinary Surgeons and Taxidermists. (Wan way or another you always get yer dug back.)'"

A GLASGOW reader was in his local at the weekend when a chap who had dodged in for a pint announced that he had only got out as he told his wife he was taking the dog for a walk.

"Where is it?" asked the barman.

The crestfallen toper realised he was no mastermind as he then muttered: "At home with the wife."

AFTER OUR story of the chap escaping to the pub by saying he was walking the dog, then forgetting to take it, Robbie Duncan tells us: "A friend in Brodick arrived home and when his wife asked him where he had been, he said he was walking the dog.

" 'That's strange because that's not our dog,' replied his wife. He had indeed popped into a local hotel for a wee tipple and left with a friend's dog by mistake."

OUR TALE of the Moscow State Circus at Braehead reminds Barry McGirr of hearing comedian Mick Miller at The Leapark

Hotel in Grangemouth recently tell the audience that he started in showbiz by running away with the circus, and was with them for nine years.

He didn't do an act, he said, but was the only one who knew how to get the tent in the bag.

DOGS' NAMES continued. Sandy Wardrope tells us: "Years back my Aunt Celia had a Skye terrier called Whisky, who was prone to doing a runner whenever the front door was left open.

"He escaped one day just before the New Year and had my aunt running after him shouting: 'Whisky, Whisky, here Whisky.'

"The nearby council bin-men heard her shouts and, excited, immediately ran towards her shouting: 'Where, where?'"

22
A Fond Farewell

Alas we had to say goodbye to some well-known folk over the year. Here are some of their stories.

SAD TO hear of the death of Celtic's Sean Fallon, Jock Stein's right-hand man. We recall the story of Stein being seriously injured in a car crash, and Fallon taking charge of the team. He visited Stein in hospital where the great man could not speak. Instead Stein scribbled in a notepad asking how the team had performed.

Fallon wrote down a reply about the team doing well and handed back the pad. Stein scribbled furiously away and wrote, with a few expletives, that, while he couldn't speak, he could still hear perfectly well.

THE GENTLEMANLY actor Richard Briers of *The Good Life* and *Monarch of the Glen* has sadly died. The story is told that when comedian Ross Noble appeared on the radio show *Just A Minute*, host Nicholas Parsons asked him who his favourite comedian was and Ross replied: "Richard Pryor," the edgy black American. He added: "What a life. Raised in a brothel, spells in jail, drink and drugs and psychological issues, nearly burned himself alive trying to freebase crack cocaine."

Later, with a look of great concern, Parsons was heard saying to another guest: "Have you heard about Richard Briers?"

IAN BROCK in Bearsden tells us about an organist at a funeral playing the rousing 'Dambusters March' as the mourners were leaving the crematorium.

When the undertaker asked why he chose the music the organist rather smugly replied that he had noticed that the deceased had a floral arrangement spelling out Biggles and assumed that was his nickname as a former RAF pilot.

The undertaker shook his head and told the organist: "You were half correct. It was a nickname – he was known as Big Les."

DAD'S ARMY actor Clive Dunn has sadly died. We remember him recounting that after the war he began his stage career – singing, dancing, telling jokes, acting, all for £8 a week. Clive added: "I found out that the washer-up at the theatre was getting £12 a week. It was Les Dawson. I could only deduce that his washing-up was funnier than my comedy act."

NOSTALGIC thoughts of televised wrestling on Saturday afternoons, Kent Walton commentaries and excitable old ladies attacking wrestlers with their umbrellas with the news that legendary grappler Mick McManus has died.

Our minds wander to when *Taggart* actor Mark McManus was

erroneously called Mick McManus on the London underground.

Without looking up from the book he was reading, the actor replied: "The name's not Mick McManus. The name's Mark McManus. Mick McManus was a wrestler – and not a very good one."

JIMMY WRAY, the colourful Gorbals lad who became a Labour MP in Glasgow's east end, has died at the age of 78.

When he was in the Commons he was paired – the system whereby opponents can both be absent at the same time – with Tory grandee Michael Heseltine.

Jimmy said at the time: "We're well matched. Heseltine is one of the 200 richest men in Britain, and I'm one of the 200 poorest."

INCIDENTALLY, Jimmy always had connections to source all sorts of things. He once arrived at Labour's annual conference in Blackpool with a safe in the back of his 4x4. He had promised to get one for a fellow MP who wanted a secure place for sensitive documents.

The only snag was it was too heavy to manhandle from Jimmy's car to his colleague's. So Jimmy just trotted round to the Blackpool tram depot where he talked them into lending him a forklift truck to carry out the safe shifting.

SADLY, Peter Gilmore, a familiar face on seventies television as the ship's master in *The Onedin Line*, has died.

Robin Gilmour tells us that at Glasgow Airport at the time, there was always a rush to the toilet when the flight to Benidorm was called, because many passengers had spent the previous couple of hours in the bar starting their holiday early with a few pints. Check-in staff dubbed the queue at the nearby loo the Oh Needin' Line.

CARL ELSENER, the designer who made the Swiss Army Knife popular around the world, has died at the age of ninety.

We remember when a female reader told us the Swiss Army Knife was definitely male. She argued: "It's male because even though it appears useful for a wide variety of work, it spends most of its time just opening bottles."

OUR STORY of the crematorium organist reminded David Rodger in Stevenston, a kirk organist, of standing in as holiday relief at the local crem. Says David: "Unfortunately, not long after playing some quiet Handel, I found myself locked in. I shouted for half an hour, to no avail.

"Not wishing to spend the weekend in such dreich surroundings

I inched my way slowly along the now motionless conveyor belt where the coffin is placed. Eventually I plopped out into what was a small ante-room, just next to the actual furnace. The three men there in dark suits seemed to get a hell of a fright."

SAD to hear of the sudden death of former Scottish Office Minister and Lord Advocate Peter Fraser, who became Lord Fraser of Carmyllie.

Despite his legal position, Lord Fraser could often be a colourful speaker. We remember when he suggested a key witness in the Lockerbie trial had often changed his testimony. Or as Peter put it: "I think even his family would say he was an apple short of a picnic."

If only today's politicians were so poetic.

THE DEATH of *Mr & Mrs* host Derek Batey reminds Glasgow writer Brian McGeachan of seeing a live theatre version of the show in Blackpool in the 1980s when then Celtic manager Davie Hay and his wife were coaxed from the audience to take part.

Says Brian: "Derek Batey innocently asked the occupation of the man standing beside his wife, Catherine. Given the high-profile nature of his occupation, it must be the only time that audience members were shouting out the answers."

SAD TO hear of the death of pub entrepreneur Brian MacDade who successfully ran the Stakis nightclubs and inns some years ago. Susan Young, publisher of the drinks magazine *Dram*, tells us Brian always told the story that, once when he was down on his luck, he was waiting at Glasgow Airport to fly north in a tiny scheduled plane to get the sack from his job. Just then a former school pal flying to London bumped into him and told him how well he was doing.

Brian feared telling the chap how badly he was doing when the pilot of the plane approached Brian and, as he was the only passenger, told him his plane was ready.

"Private jet," muttered Brian to the old school pal, and walked away with the pilot.

OPINION is divided on whether Hugo Chavez, the late Venezuelan president was a force for good or bad. One left-winger in a Glasgow pub last night was trying to impress a young woman by telling her: "Chavez was my hero. So much so that I had his initials inscribed on my bathroom taps. Do you want to come round to see them?"

THE DEATH of television astronomer Sir Patrick Moore reminds us of when he was asked if he had ever seen an Unidentified Flying Object.

"Yes, in my observatory one day. I saw a huge fleet of perfect flying saucers," was his surprising answer. He then added: "'The Martians have arrived,' I thought. Then I found out what it really was . . . pollen."

AMID the frenzied avalanche of tweets about the death of Margaret Thatcher, we noticed this one from a young person in South Ayrshire.

"Don't even know anything about this Margaret Thatcher," she tweeted shortly after news was announced, "but don't really care, my dads buzzing and taking us all out for dinner!"

WE WON'T ponder the merits or otherwise of Margaret Thatcher, but we will pass on the views of Ravenscraig shop steward Tommy Brennan who was asked on television what he thought of her after the devastation she brought to the Lanarkshire steel industry. Tommy said he did not like speaking ill of the dead but added: "I have a simple philosophy in life that if you look at every bad situation you may find a little plus there. The one plus I could find about Thatcher was that she brought salmon back to the Clyde – she closed all the industry on either side of it so they couldn't pollute it."

CRITICS were always divided on the merits of Michael Winner's films, such as *Death Wish*. As one reader told us: "I hope, as a mark of respect to Michael Winner, the television companies don't put on any of his films."

SAD TO hear of the death of leading motoring writer in Scotland, Malcolm McDougall. Always one to speak his mind, Malcolm once told racing champion Sir Jackie Stewart: "Your hair's too long – you look like a hippy." They remained friends thereafter.

Never a shy man, Malcolm was seen at Glasgow Airport where he fancied a refreshment. He merely walked into an executive lounge and announced that he was a personal friend of the airline's chairman and had been sent to check the white wine was being served at the right temperature. He was immediately served.

WE WERE all saddened by the news of astronaut Neil Armstrong's death and moved once again by the grainy television pictures of him taking the first steps on the moon.

But a keen fan of astronomy tries to cheer us up by revealing: "Apparently Armstrong used to tell bad jokes about the moon.

"When no-one laughed, he'd shrug and say, 'Guess you had to be there.'"

MAX BYGRAVES, who has sadly died, was well loved by Glasgow audiences – even those at the Glasgow Empire who were known for being tough on English acts.

But as one Glaswegian, now living in Essex, recounted: "My gran was absolutely madly in love with Max Bygraves – so much so that when she went to see him at the Empire she managed to 'acquire' the full-size cardboard cut-out of him which had adorned the foyer of the theatre.

"She simply lifted it and took the train home with Max Bygraves under her arm. It then spent years having pride of place in her house."

THE DEATH of Lanarkshire businessman and former Hamilton Accies chairman Jan Stepek reminds a reader of a works outing to Hamilton races, and the chaps stopping for a drink in the way home in a Hamilton boozer. Being peckish after a few beers, one of the crew was dispatched to find somewhere to eat, and he returned to say there was a "steak pie restaurant" across the road.

They decided he needed a trip to Specsavers when they tumbled out of the pub and read the sign across the road which stated Stepek Restorations.

23
Sport

Andy Murray winning Wimbledon, a new Scotland manager, promotion for Partick Thistle, and Rangers still in the mire – no wonder sport continued to be the big talking point in Scotland.

CONGRATULATIONS to Partick Thistle, often the butt of humour in Glasgow, on their promotion to the SPL.

We recall that even Bertie Auld, when he was Thistle manager, couldn't stop himself from announcing at the time that Thistle had a great chance of winning a major European competition that season.

He then added: "We've still to write the song though."

AFTER the news story about the Hibs match announcer being sacked for playing 'Taxman' by the Beatles, in mocking reference to rival Hearts' woes, Keith White in Paisley recalls: "The referee and two linesmen at Paisley Pirates ice-hockey match took to the ice accompanied by the tune 'Three Blind Mice'. That announcer was also reprimanded."

RUGBY tours: the two words which bring a distant smile to accountants, bankers and lawyers in Scotland. Says one of the aforementioned: "On a rugby tour to Washington DC in the 70s I made the acquaintance of a young lady.

"At a party someone asked how my voice had become so hoarse. My explanation was that it was due to 'all the shouting and bawling' I had been doing. I meant, of course, loud singing of rugby songs, but I got a serious slap from my companion before it was explained that the Scottish word 'bawling' had quite a different meaning from the American 'balling.'"

YOU GET the impression that Rangers don't command the respect they once did. Eddy Calvin was on the subway after the football when a Partick Thistle fan asked a Rangers fan what the score had been in their cup tie against lowly Alloa Athletic.

"It was 6-0 when we left," the Gers fan replied.

"Who for?" asked the Thistle fan innocently.

WE ASKED for a Commonwealth Games motto to reflect them being held in Glasgow. Ian Mouat in Glasgow suggests a local translation of the Sydney Olympics motto "Share the Spirit." In Glasgow it would be "Pass the Buckie".

VINCE BROLLY in Rutherglen suggested one which he claimed could also be used for Scotland's independence referendum. "Scotland for the high jump," says Vince.

DAVID DONALDSON harks back to the city's gang slogans of the sixties. Says David: "Since the spirit of pure amateurism seems to have degenerated into an obsession with medals won, the appropriate motto for Glasgow's Games must be: 'Gongs ya bass!'"

THE STORY of Trades House convener Colonel John Kelly being criticised for his grip despite having a hole-in-one on his first golf lesson, reminds Ian Barnett: "I was fortunate enough to get a hole-in-one at the 17th at Pollok Golf Club.

"When I put up the customary bottle, one of the old Pollok buffers came over, whisky in hand, and asked what club I used.

"Seven-iron, I told him. 'Hmmph,' he said. 'Wrong club!' And walked off."

AS PARTICK THISTLE celebrate their league win, Gordon Cubie in Bearsden recalls going in to Esquire House at Anniesland where the Thistle team were having a pre-match lunch, and meeting the then manager Bertie Auld at the door. Says Gordon: "He took one look at me and asked if I wanted a game for the first team on Saturday.

"The fact that I was hobbling on crutches with my leg in a metal caliper because of a fractured femur might have had something to do with his instant assessment of my footballing skills."

WE MUST close the turnstiles on our Partick Thistle stories, but before we do, John Neil in Stornoway reminds us of a story years ago highlighting the supposedly posher fans who follow the Jags. A woman was dropping her young son off at Firhill and shouted after him: "Don't forget to eat your sandwiches during the intermission."

CHRISTINE PACIONE recalls when her later father-in-law Emilio Pacione played for Dundee United just after the Second World War when there was no television coverage.

Says Christine: "One Saturday his family listened in vain to the radio commentary for any mention of his name. It eventually dawned on them the player frequently referred to as 'Pacy One' was in fact him!"

LET'S HOPE Gordon Strachan is successful as the new Scotland manager. We remember when he took the Celtic job that not every fan at Parkhead could be said to be in agreement. The joke told at the time was: "What have the *Titanic* and Gordon Strachan got in common?" The answer: "Neither should have left Southampton."

ON APRIL Fools' Day internet company Itison was offering tickets to the opening ceremony at Glasgow's Commonwealth Games next year for £2.50, which would be hosted by the Krankies, designed by Colin and Justin, with *River City*'s Shellsuit Bob leading a lap of honour, *Pop Idol* winner Michelle McManus singing, and First Minister Alex Salmond sky-diving into the arena.

All very amusing, although Itison's boss Oli Norman tells us that he had to divert all his staff on to answering the phones yesterday as hundreds of folk phoned wanting to buy the tickets.

TALKING of Thistle, David Speedie, currently in New York, was at Hampden in the 1960s for a Scotland international wearing his St Andrews college scarf, St Salvator's, which was black with a red and yellow stripe.

Says David: "At half time a wee man, with the exaggerated ceremony of the inebriate, wipes his half-bottle on his sleeve and hands it to me. I politely decline. Pointing to my scarf, he says, 'Take the whole bottle, pal —you need it mair than me.'"

TWO kilted Scottish fans heading to the pub to watch the Serbia v Scotland game were discussing the team's chances. The more pessimistic announced: "Gordon Strachan's had more withdrawals than a Cypriot cash dispenser."

FORMER Rangers centre-back Harold Davis, who survived being shot in the Korean War, has his biography, *Tougher Than Bullets*, published in paperback. Showing that football has perhaps changed over the years, he recalled staying on after training with fellow players Ralph Brand and Jimmy Millar to perfect some moves.

Suddenly manger Scot Symon appeared and shouted: "What the heck do you think you're doing?" When Harold explained he was doing some passing exercises, Symon snapped: "I don't want you to be a ball-player. You're a ball-winner. Get in there, have a bath and go home."

FORMER Open champion Paul Lawrie told the audience at the Prince and Princess of Wales Hospice's fundraising Sportsman's Dinner in Glasgow that he was playing in America with fellow Scots golfer Colin Montgomerie when someone in the crowd tried to attract the attention of an overweight Colin by shouting his name out.

Monty ignored the calls until the chap became more polite and shouted "Mr Montgomerie!" instead of "Colin". But as a taciturn Monty turned to acknowledge the greeting, the spectator shouted back at the full-figured golfer: "Nice tits!"

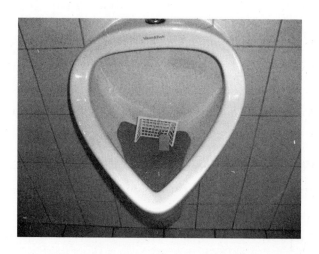

WE HAVE a postscript to St Mirren winning the League Cup. Duncan Smith watched bouncers at a Paisley pub invoking the pub's rule that football colours should not be worn on the premises. Despite the cup win they were applying the rule to St Mirren fans and not letting them in if wearing team replica strips or scarves.

Says Duncan: "I found it strange to witness one chap remove his scarf and put it in his pocket before gaining entry. What was strange? His face was painted with black and white stripes."

AH THE BANTER. Lisbon Lion Bertie Auld tells the tale in Alex Gordon's splendid history of Celtic in the 1960s, *The Awakening*, of being in the tunnel before an Old Firm game when Rangers captain John Greig told him: "Bertie, we're picking up £60 a week at Rangers these days. What are you on at Celtic?" Bertie couldn't resist replying: "Just a little bit short of that John. But then we get win bonuses and you don't."

A READER in England sees the headline "Scotland set to launch first satellite" and remarks: "Otherwise known as a 'shot on goal.'"

"I THINK Andy Murray's been away from Scotland too long," says reader Chris Lawrie in Port Glasgow. Andy wrote on his BBC blog: "I don't mind if I'm a little bit nervous the day before, because that means I know I'm going to be pumped the next day."

OUR STORY about run-down city streets reminds Hearts fan Gavin Aitchison of visiting London two weeks after the riots to see a Spurs v Hearts game. Says Gavin: "On the train to Tottenham we passed a particularly brutal area – a derelict building, graffiti galore, remains of a bonfire and some smashed windows. One of the Hearts fans asked a Spurs fan if that was where the riots had been. We were a bit taken aback when he replied, 'No, that's been like that for twenty-five years.'"

GLASGOW WARRIORS business development manager Fergus Wallace was a pretty good rugby player himself in his day, just missing out on a full international cap for Scotland. But as

Fergus told the St Andrew's Sporting Club in Glasgow: "I was often compared to the Lions great, Willie John McBride.

"Yes, folk would say to me, 'compared to Willie John McBride you're rubbish.'"

SERENA WILLIAMS won the French Open confirming her position as the top female player in the world. Glasgow actor Sanjeev Kohli from *Still Game* pondered: "Do you think Serena and Venus have a younger brother called Tennisy Williams?"

HOW time flies . . . it was ten years ago that Celtic played in the UEFA Cup final in Seville, an occasion enjoyed by thousands of Celtic fans who trekked to the Spanish city with or without tickets. We recall one Clydebank fan who was driving there with his mates, and within a couple of miles had to stop to change a flat tyre in the rain.

When he got back in the car he fished his match ticket out of his sodden pocket and realised all the print on it had run.

He quickly surmised the ticket he had bought in a Clydebank pub was a fake, shrugged his shoulders, and carried on driving.

OUR MENTION of the 10th anniversary of Celtic's cup final in Seville reminds journalist Paul Drury: "I was interviewing fans, and spoke to one who had travelled by bus all the way from Glasgow, through Scotland, England, all of France and all of Spain.

"I may have winced slightly as I asked him about going such a distance by bus and he replied, 'Naw, naw, it wiz fine – until the bogs got blocked at Bordeaux.'"

OUR TALE of the rugby player being compared to the great Willie John McBride – "compared to Willie John McBride you're rubbish" – reminds Robin Gilmour of playing in goal many years ago for the Western Hockey Club.

Says Robin: "I was flattered after a game to be called 'The Cat' by my captain.

"Sadly, one of my team-mates chipped in: 'What he really means is when the ball comes near the goal, we all have kittens.'"

"AN AUSTRALIAN, a New Zealander, a South African, a Tongan and a Samoan walk into a bar, and the barman says: 'Congratulations on being chosen for the British and Irish Lions squad to tour Australia,'" a disgruntled rugby fan phones to tell us.

LINWOOD'S Hillman Imp – snapped throttle cable anyone? – is fifty years old. We are reminded of Celtic's Lisbon Lions final when a number of Hillman Imps were driven to Portugal for the game. The story was told of two Glaswegians who hitch-hiked to the final and were sitting in a bar afterwards discussing how to get home when a chap stopped outside in his Imp.

One of the Glaswegians went over to ask him for a lift but returned to tell his pal: "Nae use tae us. He's goin' to Edinburgh."

EDINBURGH football club Hearts are in a bit of a state, with the announcement that they have put all their players up for sale as they are so short of cash.

As one fan of city rivals Hibs told us: "Their Lithuanian owner Romanov once boasted that he would make Hearts reach the level of Rangers and Celtic.

"Well he was half right."

WELL DONE St Mirren on winning the League Cup. It allows Andy Cameron to dust off a classic, okay very old, joke, when he tells us: "The Tile Bar in Paisley decided to give St Mirren fans a wee bonus for winning the cup and made every drink the same price as it was in 1959 when they beat Aberdeen 3-1 in the Scottish Cup.

"Half an hour after the doors opened the pub was empty and the owner went outside only to find a queue stretching back to Ralston. 'Come in,' he said,' the prices are all from 1959' only to be greeted with a chorus of 'Naw, we're waitin' for the happy hour.'"

ALTHOUGH the Jags are league winners, they alas have been mocked in the past. Douglas McLeod in Newlands remembers an episode of cop drama *Taggart* where the murder victim was found with no ID but was wearing a Thistle scarf.

In the mortuary a cop told the pathologist: "The only thing we know about this one is that he was a Partick Thistle supporter."

And the pathologist replied: "Well at least his suffering is over now."

WE ASKED for your Partick Thistle stories to celebrate their league triumph, and Sheriff J P Murphy recalls: "Some years ago a young Thistle fan was walking down Maryhill Road on a day the Jags were playing Rangers at home. He was approached by a Rangers supporter who asked how to get to Firhill.

" 'Just follow the crowd,' said the lad.

" 'The last time I tried to get to Firhill by doing that,' replied the Gers fan, 'I ended up in Woolworths.'"

AND NOW of course the Thistle fans are emerging from the woodwork, claiming to support the Jags despite few trips to Maryhill. As comedy writer Greg Hemphill astutely stated: "Love the Jags. They're in my blood. Nobody has pretended to support them longer than me."

MATT VALLANCE remembers *The Herald*'s great sportswriter Ian "Dan" Archer being at Firhill where his enjoyment of the game was spoiled by the Jags fan in front hurling vitriolic abuse at Thistle's Doug Somner throughout the game.

Eventually just before the end Ian tapped the abusive fan on the shoulder and informed him: "By the way pal, Doug Somner isn't playing today."

Unabashed, the fan replied: "Sorry son, it's these new glesses – ah can hardly see the field, faur less the players."

OUR STORY of the late great sports writer Ian Archer being a Partick Thistle fan reminds Barrie Crawford of Ian being the guest speaker at a referees conference and telling the tale of having to write a headline when his beloved Thistle were beaten 6-1 by Rangers.

He almost got the sack by coming up with: "Thistle in seven-goal thriller."

THE R&A has defended all-male golf clubs as it gears up for the Open in Muirfield. It reminds James Miller in Orkney of the male club captain who received a complaint from female golfers about men on the clubhouse balcony laughing at ladies playing on the 18th green.

Said Jimmy: "He told the ladies it was intolerable and promised to take action.

"Next day a new rule was posted on the noticeboard intimating that if there were men on the clubhouse balcony, the ladies could not play the 18th hole."

GREAT NEWS of course, Celtic qualifying for the last sixteen in Europe with the winning goal being scored from a penalty after striker Georgios Samaras went down in the penalty box.

Not everyone in Glasgow was impressed, however. As Jim Evans tells us: "Just to let concerned Celtic fans know that Samaras's local council has spread extra grit on the pavement outside his home just in case he goes down like a ton of bricks. Well done."

STIRLING ALBION fans had to put up with Rangers celebrating their 140th anniversary at the game between the two clubs. Frank O'Donnell heard one Stirling fan at the match sniffily remark: "I don't know what all the fuss is about Rangers taking 140 years to get to division three. It only took us two seasons."

IN a year of conspicuous highs and lows, Dundee United Football Club has asked its fans, via Facebook, for their club highlight of 2012.

One Arab, clearly not keen to allow the team's wayward form to get him down, showed where his real priorities lay: "I bought two pies, two Bovrils and a packet of cheese 'n' onion McCoys once. Did not get charged for the McCoys. Buzzing."

CELTIC'S new signing, Tunisian striker Lassad Nouioui, has a surname like a bad Scrabble hand, which has left the country's worthy sports commentators struggling with the pronunciation. A Celtic fan listening to Radio Scotland memorably described it: "Chick Young sounded like his tongue was in an arm-wrestling contest with a drunk sailor."

A Celtic spokesman has thrown the commentators a lifeline by saying the new striker likes to be known simply as Lassad.

MOTHERWELL'S Liverpudlian striker Michael Higdon was arrested for an alleged assault in a Glasgow nightclub hours after being named Scotland's Player of the Year. As a reader states: "Surely this must be enough to make Higdon eligible to play for Scotland."

A READER in his London local was listening to the news about Gordon Strachan being made Scotland manager when an English chap further up the bar said: "Strachan says he's already preparing for the 2014 World Cup." He added: "Must have bought himself a new telly."

FITBA fans were discussing the Swansea ballboy kicked by a Chelsea player for holding onto the ball too long. One fan said: "I'm surprised Paul Lambert, the Aston Villa manager, hasn't signed the ballboy – he could do with someone who can hang onto the ball for more than five seconds."

WAYWARD ballboys are nothing new. Older Dumbarton fans tell us a ballboy was sent off in the 1950s when he disagreed with a ref's decision and managed to hit the official on the napper with a carefully aimed pie.

THE SCOTTISH League Cup is now the Communities League Cup, and is sponsored by the Scottish Government, keen to promote community spirit and responsible behaviour. So at half-time in Saturday's Hearts v Inverness Caledonian Thistle semi-final, the PA announcer read a sponsor's message extolling the importance of communities and encouraging people to "behave responsibly, considerately and respectfully at all times."

"Bloody hell," Gav Aitchison heard one Hearts fan remark. "It's like having your wife at the football."

RANGERS fans of course were bragging about setting a world record for the largest crowd at any fourth tier football game. However one non-Rangers supporter at a Glasgow office loftily replied: "That's a bit like bragging about being the best-dressed man in Albania."